Math Practice Pages for the Standardized Tests Your Kids Take

Terrific Strategies and Practice Pages That Familiarize Kids With Standardized Test Formats and Help Them Tackle the Tests With Confidence

by Sara Davis Powell

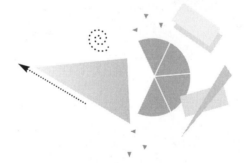

SCHOLASTIC
PROFESSIONAL BOOKS

New York • Toronto • London • Auckland • Sydney
Mexico City • New Delhi • Hong Kong • Buenos Aires

Acknowledgments

Thanks to my Scholastic editor, Joanna Davis-Swing, for her efficient manner, kind disposition, and always-on-target suggestions. My heartfelt appreciation goes to my husband, Rus, for his tireless editing, insightful advising, and ever-abundant encouragement during late-night revision sessions on our front porch. I can't imagine a more supportive friend and partner!

Cover design by Josué Castilleja
Interior design by Sydney Wright
Illustrations by Steve Cox

ISBN: 0-439-11110-2

Contents

Introduction

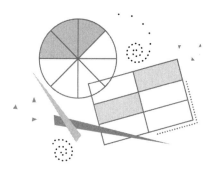

*W*e know what is expected of our students. Standards and benchmarks make it clear. We may not feel expectations are appropriately placed, but with current governmental involvement and calls for accountability, standards and their assessment are a fact of life in public education. Our responsibilities as teachers include understanding the expectations, ascertaining where our students are in terms of mastery, and then doing what we can to incorporate content and processes that will move our students in a positive direction.

The National Council of Teachers of Mathematics has developed content and process standards to guide the teaching of mathematics. With standards in place, measures of accountability are inevitable. These measures often take the form of the standardized tests we are all so familiar with. The good news is that the tests—for the most part—provide students with opportunities to exercise critical thinking as they demonstrate their mathematical abilities. As teachers, we have the responsibility to familiarize our students with testing formats so they can perform to their full potential.

Many state standardized tests go beyond the traditional multiple choice format to assess critical thinking skills. They include open-ended items that require students to show and explain the work that leads to their solutions. Although this book's tests are in multiple choice format, many of the items parallel open-ended items from state tests and can easily be transformed into practice items without four choices. Simply copy or rewrite just the questions without the choices and follow them with directions such as "Show your work," "Write a paragraph about the thinking that led to the solutions," "Give your answer and then tell why you think it is correct," or any other phrase that indicates that more than a simple answer is required.

Preparation for standardized testing should be an habitual part of our daily classroom instruction, beginning with the first week of school and continuing through final exams. It's a natural fit—our lessons are designed to promote learning, and standardized tests are designed to measure learning. It is important to remember that what we do in the name of preparation should not be disruptive or isolated. National and state expectations should be embedded in what we do in our classrooms. The features in this book will help you do just that. Read on!

Special Features

☑ Variety of Format

This book provides materials that will help our students increase their flexibility in approaching math problems. Each topic is covered in a variety of ways. For instance, students must be able to apply their understanding of multiples in the context of straightforward computation as well as in the context of a word problem. They will be asked to show their skills in recognizing and manipulating place value concepts by identifying a number in a specified place, by filling in a missing number given the spelled-out version, and by writing a standard numeral given expanded notation. Some standardized tests require a student to complete a problem one way, and some require another way. This book provides opportunities to increase your students' flexibility when confronted with a math problem, thereby increasing the depth of their understanding.

☑ Targeted Exercises by Grade Level

Many students begin learning the skills and concepts of mathematics in the very earliest formal learning settings and continue at varied paces throughout high school. All teachers acknowledge that students are at very different places in their levels of understanding of skills and content, even within the same grade and classroom. Although standards are explicit when it comes to what is to be taught and learned in specific grades, some tests dip back into fifth grade for test items for seventh graders and others seem to leap ahead to sixth grade for some fourth grade items. This book provides a sampling of what is in many grades 4 and 5 tests and also a sampling of what is in many grades 6–8 tests. Some teachers may want fifth graders to attempt the grades 6–8 exercises in certain content areas and at some point during the year. So this text offers you both specificity *and* flexibility in grade-level material.

☑ Test Specific Format

This book provides item formats used in five nationally normed tests and nine specific state tests. We have all probably observed students who know the content of what is tested, but who do the problems incorrectly simply because they are unfamiliar with the format of the question. In other words, students are actually tested on format adaptability rather than content, which is unfair. It is vital that we expose our students to the format in which a concept will be assessed.

Each set of practice exercises is preceded by a grid that links the questions to specific tests, providing a glimpse of formats used by the tests. The word *glimpse* is used to avoid misrepresenting the value of the grids. An "X" in a box indicates that at some point in the year 2000, or in the previous five years, a specific test asked students to respond in a format similar to the one represented. If an item is not marked as matching a specific test, it is not an absolute indication that the format is not used. The information used to complete the grids is from samples provided by states and practice test makers, and, in a few instances, from actual released tests used in previous years. The differing availability of sample tests accounts, in part, for the varying amount of coverage.

The tests used on the format grids include:

Nationally Normed Tests	Specific State Tests
California Achievement Test	FCAT—Florida
Iowa Test of Basic Skills	GEPA and ESPA—New Jersey
Metropolitan Achievement Test, Edition 7	ISAT—Illinois
Stanford Achievement Test, Edition 9	LEAP—Louisiana
Terra Nova	MCAS—Massachusetts
	MEAP—Michigan
	NYS—New York
	PACT—South Carolina
	TAAS—Texas

☑ Repeated Practice with Percent

As teachers, we are accustomed to exercise pages that simplify the process of obtaining a percentage grade. We typically have pages with 10, 20, 25, or 50 items. This book purposefully presents pages with 11, 17, 23, and 31 items and a space at the top for students to compute their own percentage grades. This format gives them practice with the concepts of percent, division, and rounding off. Showing students the procedure independent of a formal chapter on percent, but within a realistic context, will teach your students the value of percentages and make success on the formal percent unit more accessible to them.

☑ Teaching Tips

Each content section includes tips and suggestions for teaching what we want students to know and be able to do. Of course, the tips do not compose a comprehensive view of how to approach a topic. What they provide are ideas on what to emphasize.

☑ Super Success Strategies

Each content section includes testing strategies specific to that content. The strategies give students reminders of basic facts and skills, along with tips on how to avoid common student mistakes.

☑ National Council of Teachers of Mathematics Standards

The NCTM Standards are included at the beginning of each chapter. These standards are concise, and they are used to guide the writing of national test publications as well as state standards and assessment.

☑ Teaching and Testing Tools

Some state standardized tests give students access to specific measurement equivalents, formulas, and measuring tools right in the test booklets. You can find out if this occurs in your state by contacting your testing coordinator or obtaining released tests. The Teaching and Testing Tools section in the back of this book shows the range of tools provided in the tests spotlighted in the text.

CHAPTER 1

Number and Operations

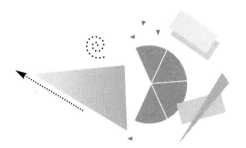

*t*he Number and Operations Standard addresses counting, numbers, and arithmetic, as well as number systems and structures. The principles involved in algebra, geometry, measurement, data analysis, and probability all require a solid understanding of number sense and fluency in computation. The largest amount of material in this book focuses on this vital standard. Topics emphasized include:

* Place Value
* Comparing Whole Numbers, Fractions, and Decimals
* Computation with Whole Numbers, Fractions, and Decimals
* Problem Solving with Whole Numbers, Fractions, and Decimals
* Computation and Problem Solving with Percent
* Ratio and Proportion
* Expanded and Scientific Notation
* Multiples and Factors
* Estimation and Rounding
* Order of Operations
* Integers

NCTM provides three standards that all students should meet to demonstrate their understanding of numbers and operations. These standards focus our instruction on helping all students:

* Understand numbers, ways of representing numbers, relationships among numbers and number systems
* Understand meaning of operations and how they relate to one another
* Compute fluently and make reasonable estimates

Following are the NCTM Standards for Number and Operations with accompanying expectations for grades 3–5 and 6–8.

Standards	Expectations
Understand numbers, ways of representing numbers, relationships among numbers, and number systems	✳ Understand the place-value structure of the base-ten number system and be able to represent and compare whole numbers and decimals; ✳ Recognize equivalent representations for the same number and generate them by decomposing and composing numbers; ✳ Develop understanding of fractions as parts of unit wholes, as parts of a collection, as locations on number lines, and as divisions of whole numbers; ✳ Use models, benchmarks, and equivalent forms to judge the size of fractions; ✳ Recognize and generate equivalent forms of commonly used fractions, decimals, and percents; ✳ Explore numbers less than 0 by extending the number line, and through familiar applications; ✳ Describe classes of numbers according to characteristics such as the nature of their factors.
Understand meanings of operations and how they relate to one another	✳ Understand various meanings of multiplication and division; ✳ Understand the effects of multiplying and dividing whole numbers; ✳ Identify and use relationships between operations, such as division as the inverse of multiplication, to solve problems; ✳ Understand and use properties of operations, such as the distributivity of multiplication over addition.
Compute fluently and make reasonable estimates	✳ Develop fluency with basic number combinations for multiplication and division and use these combinations to mentally compute related problems, such as 30×50; ✳ Develop fluency in adding, subtracting, multiplying, and dividing whole numbers; ✳ Develop and use strategies to estimate the results of whole-number computations and to judge the reasonableness of such results; ✳ Develop and use strategies to estimate computations involving fractions and decimals in situations relevant to students experiences; ✳ Use visual models, benchmarks, and equivalent forms to add and subtract commonly used fractions and decimals; ✳ Select appropriate methods and tools for computing with whole numbers from among mental computation, estimation, calculators, and paper and pencil according to the context and nature of the computation, and use the selected method or tool.

Standards	Expectations
Understand numbers, ways of representing numbers, relationships among numbers, and number systems	✳ Work flexibly with fractions, decimals, and percents to solve problems; ✳ Compare and order fractions, decimals, and percents efficiently and find their approximate locations on a number line; ✳ Develop meaning for percents greater than 100 and less than 1; ✳ Understand and use ratios and proportions to represent quantitative relationships; ✳ Develop an understanding of large numbers and recognize and appropriately use exponential, scientific, and calculator notation; ✳ Use factors, multiples, prime factorization, and relatively prime numbers to solve problems; ✳ Develop meaning for integers and represent and compare quantities with them.
Understand meanings of operations and how they relate to one another	✳ Understand the meaning and effects of arithmetic operations with fractions, decimals, and integers; ✳ Use the associative and commutative properties of addition and multiplication and the distributive property of multiplication over addition to simplify computations with integers, fractions, and decimals; ✳ Understand and use the inverse relationships of addition and subtraction, multiplication and division, and squaring and finding square roots to simplify computations and solve problems.
Compute fluently and make reasonable estimates	✳ Select appropriate methods and tools for computing with fractions and decimals from among mental computation, estimation, calculators, and paper and pencil depending on the situation, and apply the selected methods; ✳ Develop, and analyze algorithms for computing with fractions, decimals, and integers and develop fluency in their use; ✳ Develop and use strategies to estimate the results of rational-number computations and judge the reasonableness of the results; ✳ Develop, analyze and explain methods for solving problems involving proportions, such as scaling and finding equivalent ratios.

Place Value

*t*he notion of place value is the basis on which all computation rests. It is the fundamental understanding necessary to adequately perform operations on whole numbers, integers, and rational numbers expressed as decimals. Too often, students follow algorithms to solve problems that are in particular formats, but are lost when a slightly different format appears that requires them to alter the familiar algorithm. They are often lost because they never understood place value. For example, students may follow the traditional subtraction algorithm to solve 28.0 − .6, but may rewrite the problem as $\begin{array}{r} 28 \\ -.6 \\ \hline \end{array}$ due to a failure to understand place value.

Although it may seem simplistic, *we must emphasize place value*, even in grades 4–8. This section presents a variety of ways students may encounter place value concepts.

TEACHING TIPS

1. Display a place value diagram from hundred thousandths to millions in the classroom.

2. Give students cards with single-digit numerals printed on them. Ask students to arrange themselves to form a number that is either read to them or printed in words.

3. Provide lots of practice for students to read orally very large and very small decimal numbers, prompting them to say the decimals as "and."

4. Require students occasionally to write answers in expanded notation.

Place Value

1. When you see a number with a decimal, *read the number to yourself.*

2. Keep in mind that numbers approaching the decimal *from the left represent smaller and smaller amounts* and numbers approaching the decimal *from the right indicate increasing value* as you move from one place to the next.

3. Remember that *the decimal and the ones place are in the "middle."* Then on either side we begin with tens and tenths, hundreds and hundredths, and so on.

4. *Practice thinking* of an 8 in the hundreds position as 800, not just 8. A 5 in the ten thousandths position is .0005, not just 5.

5. When you write or read expanded notation, the *zeroes are place holders* that represent a place value.

Place Value (4, 5)

	page 13								
Test	1	2	3	4	5	6	7	8	9
CAT		X							
IOWA	X		X	X	X				
MAT7	X								
SAT9						X	X	X	
MCAS	X								X
NYS						X			
TAAS						X			

Place Value (6, 7, 8)

	page 14								
Test	1	2	3	4	5	6	7	8	9
IOWA						X			
MAT7						X			
SAT9						X		X	
FCAT						X		X	
ISAT		X							X
LEAP	X	X	X	X		X	X		
MCAS	X								
MEAP	X	X	X	X		X	X		

Grades 4–5

Place Value

The 5 is in the hundreds place . . .

Choose the correct answer to each problem.

1. Which numeral is *three thousand, five hundred six*?

(A) 3056   (C) 3506

(B) 3560   (D) 30,506

2. Which answer is the same as the number in the place value chart?

1000's	100's	10's	1's
3	0	7	9

(F) 379

(G) 307.9

(H) 3000 + 700 + 90

(J) Three thousand seventy nine

3. Which number has the least value?

(A) 2631   (C) 6213

(B) 1326   (D) 3216

4. If the 4 in 34,630 is changed to a 7, how much does the value of the number change?

(F) 2000   (H) 4000

(G) 3000   (J) 5000

5. Which numeral has a value between 3640 and 3730?

(A) 3590   (C) 3650

(B) 3630   (D) 3740

6. What is the value of 4 in 326.084?

(F) 4 hundreds   (H) 4 hundredths

(G) 4 thousands   (J) 4 thousandths

7. Which digit is in the hundredths place in 147.283?

(A) 1   (C) 8

(B) 2   (D) 3

8. Which number has a 5 in the thousands place and a 2 in the tenths place?

(F) 35,614.297   (H) 5462.78

(G) 46,579.23   (J) 50,392.64

9. Which number does NOT equal 236?

(A) Two hundred, 2 tens, 16 ones

(B) Two hundred, 36 tens

(C) Two hundred, 36 ones

(D) Two hundreds, 3 tens, 6 ones

Grades 6–8

Place Value

Choose the correct answer to each problem.

The 3 is in the hundredths place . . .

1. Which number is forty thousand more than 8,230,419?
   - (A) 8,234,419
   - (C) 8,630,419
   - (B) 8,270,419
   - (D) 8,230,819

2. What digit is in the thousands place in the product of 849 x 18?
   - (F) 1
   - (H) 8
   - (G) 2
   - (J) 5

3. In 81,709, which place value contains a prime number?
   - (A) thousands
   - (C) tens
   - (B) hundreds
   - (D) ones

4. What would 600 + 90 + 3 + .2 + .007 be in standard form?
   - (F) 693.27
   - (H) 693.207
   - (G) 69,327
   - (J) 600,903.2007

5. Choose another way to write 70,063.401.
   - (A) 70,000 + 60 + 3 + .4 + .01
   - (B) 70,000 + 60 + 3 + .4 + .001
   - (C) 7,000,000 + 60 + 3 + .4 + .01
   - (D) 70,000,000 + 60,000 + 3000 + 400 + 1

6. Which number represents two hundred fifty and sixty four thousandths?
   - (F) 250.64
   - (H) 250.0064
   - (G) 250.064
   - (J) 25.064

7. If the digit in the hundred-thousands place in 9,362,048 is changed to a 7, how is the value of the number affected?
   - (A) increased by 4
   - (B) decreased by 4
   - (C) increased by 40,000
   - (D) increased by 400,000

8. Mr. Parsons values accuracy in his students' lab work. During a chemistry lab, Jeremiah measured a liquid and recorded it as measuring 2.560 liters. What is the value of the 6 in this measurement?
   - (F) 6 tenths
   - (H) 6 thousandths
   - (G) 6 hundredths
   - (J) 60 hundredths

9. Which number is forty thousand more than 8,231,906?
   - (A) 8,631,906
   - (C) 8,271,906
   - (B) 8,235,906
   - (D) 12,231,906

Comparing Whole Numbers, Fractions, and Decimals

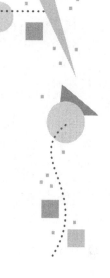

*S*tudents must know how to compare whole numbers and integers within the systems of fractions and decimals. They should be able to put whole numbers, fractions, and decimals in order from least to greatest and from greatest to least. In addition to being fluent *within* each system, students need a working knowledge of how whole numbers, fractions, and decimals *compare to each other*. The ability to make comparisons across systems will help them succeed in subsequent math courses as well as in real life, where math dilemmas often require more than one system (if a sale item is $\frac{1}{3}$ off, how much will it cost in dollars and cents?).

TEACHING TIPS

1. Display a number line in the classroom and refer to it often.

2. Create a "human number line" by giving students cards with whole numbers, fractions, and decimal numbers written on them; then ask students to arrange themselves in order from least to greatest.

3. Tie discussions of whole numbers and decimal numbers to place value concepts.

4. Encourage students to mentally picture fractional parts of objects and familiar polygons. The goal is to develop common sense that tells them, for instance, that $\frac{3}{4}$ of something is greater than $\frac{3}{8}$ of it. They should automatically recognize that fourths are larger than eighths.

5. Use manipulatives to demonstrate the underlying concept of converting fractions with unlike denominators to fractions with common denominators, so their relative values can be compared easily.

6. Make the inequality symbols $<$, $\leq$, $>$, and $\geq$ as comfortable to use as $=$.

SUPER SUCCESS STRATEGIES

Comparing Numbers

1. Always use *common sense* when comparing numbers.

2. Think about where numbers would be on a *number line* when you use "greater than" and "less than."

3. When you compare fractions, always rewrite them with *common denominators* before comparing.

4. When you compare decimal numbers, *start with the digit in the largest place value* and go to the right until the digits are different.

5. If you are asked to put numbers in order, make sure to *read carefully* "least to greatest" or "greatest to least" before you start working.

6. When comparing amounts in word problems, change all labels to the *same unit.* For instance, in a problem about time, you would change hours to minutes if another part of the problem were about minutes.

Comparing Whole Numbers, Fractions, and Decimals (4–5)

Test	pages 18–19																		page 20					
	1	2	3	4	5	6	7	8	9	10	11	12	13	14	15	16	17	18	1	2	3	4	5	6
CAT	X									X	X	X	X	X			X	X						
IOWA															X	X								
MAT7	X	X	X	X	X	X	X	X	X															
SAT9										X		X				X	X	X	X	X				
Terra					X	X																X	X	
FCAT																								X
ESPA																								
ISAT																								
LEAP																								X
MCAS																X								
MEAP																								
NYS	X						X								X							X	X	
PACT																					X	X		X
TAAS		X	X				X															X		

16

Comparing Whole Numbers, Fractions, and Decimals (6–8)

	pages 21–22															
Test	1	2	3	4	5	6	7	8	9	10	11	12	13	14	15	16
CAT					X						X					
IOWA						X		X								
MAT7	X													X	X	
SAT9																X
Terra		X					X		X							
FCAT																
GEPA				X			X			X			X			
ISAT	X									X		X				
LEAP		X								X		X				
MCAS	X															
MEAP										X		X				
NYS																
PACT																
TAAS	X														X	

Grades 4–5

Comparing Whole Numbers, Fractions, and Decimals

$\frac{1}{4}, \frac{1}{2}, \frac{3}{4}\ldots$

Choose the correct answer to each problem.

1. What part of this figure is shaded?

   Ⓐ 0.037   Ⓒ 3.70

   Ⓑ 0.37   Ⓓ 37

2. Which shaded part of the figures is the largest fraction?

   Ⓕ L   Ⓗ N

   Ⓖ M   Ⓙ P

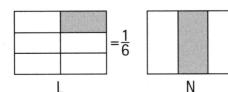

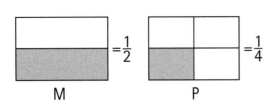

3. Which shaded part of the circles shows the smallest fraction?

   Ⓐ M   Ⓒ P

   Ⓑ N   Ⓓ Q

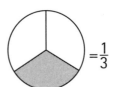 $=\frac{1}{3}$ 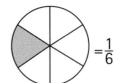 $=\frac{1}{6}$

M   P

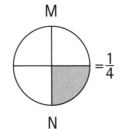 $=\frac{1}{4}$ 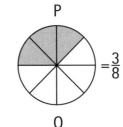 $=\frac{3}{8}$

N   Q

4. Which number fits in the ____?

  254 > ____

   Ⓕ 300   Ⓗ 254

   Ⓖ 255   Ⓙ 253

5. Which number is odd?

   Ⓐ 429   Ⓒ 390

   Ⓑ 172   Ⓓ 756

6. Which number is even?

   Ⓕ 263   Ⓗ 574

   Ⓖ 689   Ⓙ 365

7. Which decimal shows how much of this group of boxes is shaded?

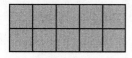 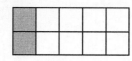

(A) 1.12   (C) 1.02
(B) 1.2   (D) 1.8

8. What fraction of an hour is 15 minutes?

(F) $\frac{1}{15}$ (H) $\frac{1}{5}$

(G) $\frac{1}{6}$ (J) $\frac{1}{4}$

9. What fraction of 1 foot is 4 inches?

(A) $\frac{1}{3}$ (C) $\frac{1}{4}$

(B) $\frac{4}{1}$ (D) $\frac{1}{4}$

10. What number goes in the _____ below the number line?

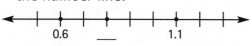

(F) 1.0   (H) 0.8
(G) 0.9   (J) 0.10

11. Which improper fraction equals $2\frac{5}{6}$?

(A) $\frac{12}{6}$ (C) $\frac{17}{6}$

(B) $\frac{25}{6}$ (D) $\frac{7}{6}$

12. Which of these fractions is written in lowest terms?

(F) $\frac{2}{5}$ (H) $\frac{2}{6}$

(G) $\frac{12}{50}$ (J) $\frac{22}{40}$

13. Which number is greater than 4693 and less than 5041?

(A) 4692   (C) 5042
(B) 4694   (D) 5060

14. Which group of fractions is in order from greatest to least?

(F) $\frac{1}{7}, \frac{1}{9}, \frac{1}{4}$ (H) $\frac{1}{9}, \frac{1}{4}, \frac{1}{7}$

(G) $\frac{1}{9}, \frac{1}{7}, \frac{1}{4}$ (J) $\frac{1}{4}, \frac{1}{7}, \frac{1}{9}$

15. Henry is waiting in line for concert tickets. He is eighth in line. How many people are in front of him?

(A) 4   (C) 6
(B) 5   (D) 7

16. $\frac{10}{24}$ of this figure is shaded. What fraction is *not* shaded?

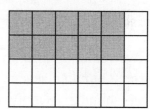

(F) $\frac{14}{24}$ (H) $\frac{3}{4}$

(G) $\frac{1}{2}$ (J) $\frac{12}{24}$

17. $\frac{12}{16}$ is the same as _____

(A) $\frac{2}{6}$ (C) $\frac{3}{4}$

(B) $\frac{5}{8}$ (D) $\frac{1}{6}$

18. $\frac{63}{9} =$

(F) 7   (H) 11
(G) 9   (J) 13

Grades 4–5

Comparing Whole Numbers, Fractions, and Decimals

$\frac{3}{4}$, is the same as .75

Choose the correct answer to each problem.

1. A science experiment involved measuring water remaining in test tubes. Hillary's tube contained 5.75 ml, Jan's tube contained 5.46 ml, Jessica's tube contained 5.69 ml, and Rose's tube contained 5.74 ml. Which girl's tube contained the most water?
- Ⓐ Hillary
- Ⓒ Jessica
- Ⓑ Jan
- Ⓓ Rose

2. How would you write 126,307 in words?
- Ⓕ Twelve hundred six thousand three hundred seven
- Ⓖ One hundred twenty-six thousand three hundred seventy
- Ⓗ One hundred twenty-six thousand three hundred seven
- Ⓙ One million twenty-six thousand three hundred seven

3. Brett's town had a great deal of snow this year. In December 2.5 feet fell, in January 3.7 feet fell, in February 2.1 feet fell, and in March 3.4 feet fell. In which month did the most snow fall?
- Ⓐ December
- Ⓒ February
- Ⓑ January
- Ⓓ March

4. Clover Elementary students sold 1632 raffle tickets in week 1; 986 tickets in week 2; 1599 tickets in week 3; and 1659 tickets in week 4. Which of these choices shows the numbers from greatest to least?
- Ⓕ 986   1599   1632   1659
- Ⓖ 1659   1599   1632   986
- Ⓗ 1632   1599   1659   986
- Ⓙ 1659   1632   1599   986

5. Between what two whole numbers would we find $\frac{5}{2}$ on the number line?

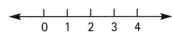

0   1   2   3   4

- Ⓐ 1 and 2
- Ⓒ 3 and 4
- Ⓑ 2 and 3
- Ⓓ 0 and 1

6. Place the numbers in order from least to greatest:
14.38, 14.08, 14.801, 14.8
- Ⓕ 14.801, 14.38, 14.08, 14.8
- Ⓖ 14.08, 14.8, 14.38, 14.801
- Ⓗ 14.38, 14.8, 14.08, 14.801
- Ⓙ 14.08, 14.38, 14.8, 14.801

Grades 6–8

Comparing Whole Numbers, Fractions, and Decimals

$\frac{1}{2}$ is greater than $\frac{1}{4}$...

Choose the correct answer for each problem.

1. Which number is represented by G on the number line?

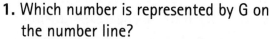

(A) 2.6   (C) 3.5

(B) 3.2   (D) 4.1

2. Which point on the number line corresponds to $2\frac{3}{4}$?

(F) L   (H) N

(G) M   (J) P

3. Which number is greatest?

(A) 3   (C) $\frac{7}{2}$

(B) $\frac{7}{3}$ (D) .72

4. Which fraction is greatest?

(F) $\frac{5}{6}$ (H) $\frac{1}{2}$

(G) $\frac{2}{3}$ (J) $\frac{5}{7}$

5. Which of the following is greater than 4.361 but less than 4.370?

(A) 4.369   (C) 4.299

(B) 4.372   (D) 4.360

6. Which decimal number has a greater value than 0.476?

(F) 0.3   (H) 0.4

(G) 0.467   (J) 0.5

7. Which is *not* equal to the others?

(A) 2.6   (C) $\frac{26}{10}$

(B) $2\frac{1}{6}$ (D) 260%

8. Which fraction represents the smallest quantity?

(F) $\frac{1}{4}$ (H) $\frac{1}{6}$

(G) $\frac{1}{5}$ (J) $\frac{1}{7}$

9. Which number makes the number sentence true?

$$700.06 > \underline{\hspace{1cm}}$$

(A) 701   (C) 700.07

(B) 700.006   (D) 706

10. Which value of X makes this statement true?

$$6.2 < x < 6.9$$

Ⓕ 6.4 Ⓗ 6.06
Ⓖ 6.04 Ⓙ 6.96

11. Which fraction fits in the blank if they are in order from greatest to least?

$$\frac{3}{5}, \frac{1}{3}, \underline{\quad}, \frac{1}{6}$$

Ⓐ $\frac{2}{5}$ Ⓒ $\frac{2}{3}$
Ⓑ $\frac{3}{10}$ Ⓓ $\frac{1}{10}$

12. Which group of decimal numbers is in order from least to greatest?

Ⓕ 3.09, 3.7, 3.62, 3.6009
Ⓖ 3.7, 3.09, 3.62, 3.6009
Ⓗ 3.09, 3.6009, 3.62, 3.7
Ⓙ 3.6009, 3.62, 3.09, 3.7

13. In a book on science experiments designed to compare the effects of amounts of sunshine on plant growth, Consuelo read that plant L grew $2\frac{3}{4}$ inches, plant M grew $2\frac{9}{10}$ inches, plant N grew $2\frac{1}{2}$ inches, and plant P grew $2\frac{7}{8}$ inches. Which plant grew the most?

Ⓐ L Ⓒ N
Ⓑ M Ⓓ P

14. Four brothers decided to measure their heights on a door jam, make pencil marks on the wood, and write their names next to their marks. From the floor, Jesse's mark was $5\frac{2}{3}$ feet,

Cody's mark was $5\frac{5}{6}$ feet, Travis' mark was $5\frac{1}{2}$ feet, and Noah's mark was $5\frac{3}{4}$ feet. From bottom to top, how were the marks labeled?

Ⓕ Jesse, Cody, Travis, Noah
Ⓖ Noah, Jesse, Cody, Travis
Ⓗ Travis, Noah, Cody, Jesse
Ⓙ Travis, Jesse, Noah, Cody

15. Four separate science experiments called for the use of iodine. The first called for 3.6 cubic centimeters, the second called for 3.54 cubic centimeters, the third called for 3.06 cubic centimeters, and the fourth called for 3.45 cubic centimeters. How would these four measurements be listed from greatest to least?

Ⓐ 3.6, 3.54, 3.45, 3.06
Ⓑ 3.06, 3.6, 3.45, 3.54
Ⓒ 3.54, 3.45, 3.6, 3.06
Ⓓ 3.06, 3.45, 3.54, 3.6

16. Kenji is interested in rocks and minerals. He has a collection of geodes that vary in size and weight. The geode from Colorado weighs $\frac{2}{3}$ pound, the one from Wyoming weighs $\frac{5}{6}$ pound, the one from Utah weighs $\frac{3}{4}$ pound, and the one from Idaho weighs $\frac{5}{8}$ pound. Which series of numbers shows the weights of the geodes from least to greatest?

Ⓕ $\frac{3}{4}, \frac{2}{3}, \frac{5}{6}, \frac{5}{8}$ Ⓗ $\frac{5}{8}, \frac{2}{3}, \frac{3}{4}, \frac{5}{6}$
Ⓖ $\frac{2}{3}, \frac{5}{6}, \frac{5}{8}, \frac{3}{4}$ Ⓙ $\frac{5}{6}, \frac{3}{4}, \frac{2}{3}, \frac{5}{8}$

Computation with Whole Numbers, Fractions, and Decimals

While teachers have not been emphasizing computation outside problem-solving scenarios in recent years, common sense tells us that a lack of basic computational skills will prevent students from correctly solving problems within a context. Performing all four basic operations with whole numbers is a component of standardized testing in grades 4–8. The degree to which these basic operations are tested using fractional and decimal numbers depends on both the grade level and the tests given.

TEACHING TIPS

1. Provide daily practice with computation.

2. Use computation problems in games and activities.

3. Regardless of the topic or unit being taught, spiral back to basic operations in class and homework assignments.

4. Be a diagnostician! Look for mistakes, especially consistent ones, and help students recognize patterns in their errors and areas that need extra review or practice.

5. Require students to often compute answers without a calculator.

Computation

1. *Don't be overwhelmed* by a whole page of computation problems. Just do them one at a time!

2. If an addition, subtraction, or multiplication problem with whole or decimal numbers is written vertically in your test booklet, just *slide a piece of scratch paper* up to the problem and work it, writing the solution on the scratch page. Copying the entire problem on to your paper takes up time, and you may even copy it incorrectly.

3. If whole or decimal numbers in an addition or subtraction problem are written horizontally, rewrite them vertically and *line up the digits* according to place value.

4. *Rewrite whole or decimal number division problems* on your own paper to work them. Change problems written with the "÷" sign to problems written with the " $\overline{)}$ " symbol.

5. Remember that you can't divide by a number (the divisor) until you make it a whole number by *moving the decimal all the way to the right*. Then move the decimal in the dividend the same number of places.

6. When multiplying decimals, your *product* should have the *same number of digits* to the right of the decimal as the sum of both of your factors' digits that are on the right of the decimal.

7. When adding or subtracting fractions and mixed numbers, you *must rewrite* the fractions so they have common denominators.

8. *Do not rewrite fractions* to have common denominators when multiplying or dividing.

9. Change *mixed numbers to improper fractions* to multiply and divide.

10. To *divide fractions*, multiply the first one by the *reciprocal* of the second one.

11. Always put answers in *simplest form*.

Computation with Whole Numbers, Fractions, and Decimals (4–5)

Test	pages 26–27																						
	1	2	3	4	5	6	7	8	9	10	11	12	13	14	15	16	17	18	19	20	21	22	23
CAT	X	X	X	X	X	X		X	X	X	X	X	X	X	X	X		X	X				
IOWA	X	X	X	X	X	X			X	X	X	X	X	X	X				X	X	X		
MAT7	X	X	X	X	X	X	X	X	X	X	X	X	X	X	X	X	X					X	
SAT9	X	X	X							X	X				X								
Terra			X							X		X	X		X								
FCAT				X									X					X			X		
ESPA	X	X			X								X		X			X			X		
ISAT																							
LEAP																							
MCAS	X	X	X	X										X				X		X			
MEAP																							
NYS	X	X																					
PACT														X				X		X			X
TAAS			X	X				X	X	X												X	

Computation with Whole Numbers, Fractions, and Decimals (6–8)

Test	pages 28–29																						
	1	2	3	4	5	6	7	8	9	10	11	12	13	14	15	16	17	18	19	20	21	22	23
CAT		X	X				X	X	X	X		X			X	X	X	X					
IOWA		X	X		X	X		X		X				X	X			X					
MAT7	X			X		X				X								X					
SAT9	X	X			X	X				X		X						X					
Terra											X												
FCAT																							
GEPA																							
ISAT																					X	X	
LEAP																					X	X	X
MCAS													X						X				
MEAP																					X	X	X
NYS																				X			
PACT						X				X								X			X		
TAAS								X					X							X			

Grades 4–5

Computation with Whole Numbers, Fractions, and Decimals

The divisor is 4, so . . .

Choose the correct answer to each problem.

1. $2\overline{)157}$

   Ⓐ 78 R1   © 78

   Ⓑ 73 R1   Ⓓ Not given

2. $6\overline{)4074}$

   Ⓕ 678   Ⓗ 679

   Ⓖ 610   Ⓙ Not given

3.   36
    x24

   Ⓐ 424   © 1224

   Ⓑ 504   Ⓓ Not given

4.   178
    x 30

   Ⓕ 534   Ⓗ 32,124

   Ⓖ 5340   Ⓙ Not given

5. 7 x ___ = 56

   Ⓐ 8   © 63

   Ⓑ 53   Ⓓ Not given

6. 47 + ___ = 76

   Ⓕ 29   Ⓗ 123

   Ⓖ 39   Ⓙ Not given

7. 58 – ___ = 32

   Ⓐ 22   © 90

   Ⓑ 26   Ⓓ Not given

8. 73.2 – 0.6 = ___

   Ⓕ 71.06   Ⓗ 73.6

   Ⓖ 73.4   Ⓙ Not given

9. $12.49
   – 5.32

   Ⓐ $17.72   © $7.26

   Ⓑ $8.26   Ⓓ Not given

10. 5.4 + 7.9 = ___

   Ⓕ 2.5   Ⓗ 13.3

   Ⓖ 12.3   Ⓙ Not given

11. $\dfrac{1}{7} + \dfrac{3}{4} =$

   Ⓐ $\dfrac{3}{49}$ © $\dfrac{4}{7}$

   Ⓑ $\dfrac{4}{14}$ Ⓓ Not given

12. $\frac{6}{7} - \frac{3}{7} =$

(F) $\frac{3}{7}$ (H) $\frac{18}{49}$

(G) $\frac{9}{7}$ (J) Not given

13. 2546
+9205

(A) 11,741 (C) 7341

(B) 11,751 (D) Not given

14. $34\overline{)2851}$

(F) 84 R5 (H) 83 R29

(G) 84 R15 (J) Not given

15. 678
−247

(A) 431 (C) 331

(B) 425 (D) Not given

16. $\frac{1}{2}$
$+\frac{2}{5}$

(F) $\frac{3}{7}$ (H) $\frac{3}{5}$

(G) $\frac{2}{5}$ (J) Not given

17. $\frac{63}{7} =$

(A) 7 (C) 11

(B) 9 (D) Not given

18. 4239
523
+ 64

(F) 4826 (H) 4726

(G) 4816 (J) Not given

19. $\frac{3}{10} + \frac{1}{10} + \frac{5}{10} =$

(A) $\frac{9}{30}$ (C) $\frac{15}{10}$

(B) $\frac{9}{10}$ (D) Not given

20. 36 x 5000 = ___

(F) 18,000 (H) 180,000

(G) 15,000 (J) Not given

21. 18
93
46
+22

(A) 169 (C) 189

(B) 170 (D) Not given

22. $34.96
+46.13

(F) $81.09 (H) $80.89

(G) $80.09 (J) Not given

23. 563
−327

(A) 244 (C) 290

(B) 236 (D) Not given

Name _____

Grades 6–8

Computation with Whole Numbers, Fractions, and Decimals

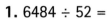

$\frac{3}{6}$ reduces to $\frac{1}{2}$

Choose the correct answer for each problem.

1. 6484 ÷ 52 =
- Ⓐ 124
- Ⓒ 126
- Ⓑ 124 $\frac{1}{2}$
- Ⓓ Not given

2. 27.16 + 39.89 =
- Ⓕ 67.05
- Ⓗ 66.73
- Ⓖ 66.95
- Ⓙ Not given

3. 0.84 – 0.17 =
- Ⓐ .067
- Ⓒ 6.7
- Ⓑ .67
- Ⓓ Not given

4. 2.425 x 3.7 =
- Ⓕ 8.9725
- Ⓗ 897.25
- Ⓖ 89.725
- Ⓙ Not given

5.   47
    x 0.26
- Ⓐ .1222
- Ⓒ 12.22
- Ⓑ 1.222
- Ⓓ Not given

6. 0.234 ÷ .09 =
- Ⓕ 2.6
- Ⓗ 0.026
- Ⓖ 0.26
- Ⓙ Not given

7. $\frac{3}{8} + \frac{1}{4}$ =
- Ⓐ $\frac{3}{32}$
- Ⓒ $\frac{4}{12}$
- Ⓑ $\frac{5}{8}$
- Ⓓ Not given

8. $\frac{1}{6} + \frac{4}{6} + \frac{7}{6}$ =
- Ⓕ $\frac{12}{18}$
- Ⓗ 2
- Ⓖ $\frac{2}{6}$
- Ⓙ Not given

9. $2\frac{2}{3} + 7\frac{5}{6}$ =
- Ⓐ $9\frac{3}{6}$
- Ⓒ $10\frac{1}{2}$
- Ⓑ $9\frac{7}{9}$
- Ⓓ Not given

10. $\frac{5}{6} - \frac{3}{8}$ =
- Ⓕ $\frac{15}{48}$
- Ⓗ $\frac{11}{24}$
- Ⓖ $\frac{2}{6}$
- Ⓙ Not given

11. 326 – 2.93 =
- Ⓐ 324.07
- Ⓒ 32.307
- Ⓑ 32.407
- Ⓓ 323.07

12. $21\frac{4}{7} - 6\frac{1}{7} =$

   Ⓕ 14.37   Ⓗ $27\frac{5}{7}$

   Ⓖ $15\frac{3}{7}$ Ⓙ Not given

13. Compute 59.3 + 18.9 – 13.04.
What is the answer?

   Ⓐ 55.16   Ⓒ 65.24

   Ⓑ 65.16   Ⓓ 91.24

14. $\frac{4}{5} \times \frac{5}{12} =$

   Ⓕ $\frac{20}{17}$ Ⓗ $\frac{25}{48}$

   Ⓖ $\frac{1}{3}$ Ⓙ Not given

15. $2\frac{1}{3} \times 3\frac{6}{7} =$

   Ⓐ $6\frac{3}{7}$ Ⓒ $7\frac{6}{21}$

   Ⓑ $6\frac{7}{10}$ Ⓓ 9

16. $\frac{1}{4} \div \frac{3}{5} =$

   Ⓕ $\frac{1}{5}$ Ⓗ $\frac{3}{20}$

   Ⓖ $\frac{5}{12}$ Ⓙ Not given

17. $11\frac{1}{3} \div \frac{4}{9} =$

   Ⓐ $25\frac{1}{2}$ Ⓒ $11\frac{5}{12}$

   Ⓑ $5\frac{1}{27}$ Ⓓ Not given

18. $\frac{9}{10} \div 5 =$

   Ⓕ $\frac{9}{50}$ Ⓗ $\frac{45}{50}$

   Ⓖ $\frac{45}{10}$ Ⓙ Not given

19. Which of these fractions converts to
a terminating decimal number?

   Ⓐ $\frac{2}{3}$ Ⓒ $\frac{4}{7}$

   Ⓑ $\frac{3}{8}$ Ⓓ $\frac{7}{9}$

20. Which fraction is equivalent to $\frac{3}{4}$?

   Ⓕ $\frac{3}{8}$ Ⓗ $\frac{9}{16}$

   Ⓖ $\frac{1}{2}$ Ⓙ $\frac{6}{8}$

21. What is the reciprocal of * ?

   Ⓐ * ÷ 1   Ⓒ 1 ÷ *

   Ⓑ (*) (1)   Ⓓ 1 – *

22. The reciprocal of .7 is ___ .

   Ⓕ $1\frac{3}{7}$ Ⓗ $\frac{7}{1}$

   Ⓖ $\frac{7}{10}$ Ⓙ $\frac{1}{7}$

23. What is the reciprocal of $3\frac{1}{4}$?

   Ⓐ $3\frac{4}{1}$ Ⓒ $\frac{13}{4}$

   Ⓑ $\frac{4}{13}$ Ⓓ $4\frac{1}{3}$

Problem Solving with Whole Numbers, Fractions, and Decimals

*p*roblem solving is the process by which we use available information to answer a question. The skill is not limited to mathematics; students should be able to apply problem-solving techniques to a variety of situations. Problem solving requires flexibility and the ability to draw upon a range of strategies, devise an appropriate approach, and work through the necessary steps in a logical manner.

Problem solving is an important part of standardized math tests and requires a strong foundation in basic computation with whole numbers, fractions, and decimals. Fluency in this type of computation will allow students to concentrate on the reasoning and logic required to successfully solve more advanced problems.

TEACHING TIPS

1. Remind students to read a problem scenario at least twice before thinking about solving it.

2. Tackle problem solving frequently as a class.

3. Think aloud for students so they can hear the steps you take to find a solution. Model logical thinking!

4. Share problem-solving approaches and aids with your students. Display reminders of the approaches in Super Success Strategy #4 below in your classroom.

5. Help students break down complex scenarios so they see how they can apply skills they already have to reach a solution.

Problem Solving

1. Read the problem once. *Read it again.* Now read it again.

2. Decide *what is given* to you in the problem.

3. What are you being asked to do? *Make sure you understand the question.*

4. There are many ways to approach a problem.
Use one or more of these:

> ✓ Restate the problem in your own words.
>
> ✓ Look for a pattern.
>
> ✓ Create a table or chart.
>
> ✓ "Picture" what's going on in the problem.
>
> ✓ Make a drawing or diagram.
>
> ✓ Make an estimate and then work out the details.
>
> ✓ Work backwards if it makes more sense.
>
> ✓ Apply a formula.

5. Once you get a solution, *think it through again* to make sure it is *reasonable and complete.*

Problem Solving with Whole Numbers, Fractions, Decimals (4–5)

Test	1	2	3	4	5	6	7	8	9	10	11	12	13	14	15	16	17	18	19	20
CAT			X			X			X	X										
IOWA			X		X	X		X	X											
MAT7	X	X	X	X	X	X	X	X	X											
SAT9			X		X	X			X		X	X	X							
Terra								X			X	X			X				X	X
FCAT												X								
ESPA	X																		X	
ISAT																				
LEAP																	X	X		
MCAS									X											
MEAP																	X	X		
NYS																			X	
PACT														X						
TAAS	X									X	X		X		X	X	X			

Problem Solving with Whole Numbers, Fractions, Decimals (6–8)

Test	1	2	3	4	5	6	7	8	9	10	11	12	13	14
CAT														X
IOWA		X						X						
MAT7											X	X	X	
SAT9		X						X					X	
Terra						X	X							
FCAT									X					
GEPA						X					X			
ISAT					X									
LEAP	X													
MCAS					X									
MEAP	X													
NYS										X				
PACT							X							X
TAAS			X	X	X	X	X						X	

Grades 4–5

Problem Solving with Whole Numbers, Fractions, and Decimals

Adding 15, 18, and 21 ...

Choose the correct answer for each problem.

1. Mr. Chang's class is selling raffle tickets for $3 each for the fall school carnival. To make the raffle sale more interesting, Mr. Chang made it a contest between the boys and the girls. If the boys sold 42 tickets and the girls sold 54 tickets, how much money did the students collect altogether?

Ⓐ $96　　Ⓒ $288

Ⓑ $99　　Ⓓ 297

2. Angela bought notebook paper for 39¢ and a red pen for 45¢. If she gave the clerk $1.00 and he didn't charge her tax, how much change did she receive?

Ⓕ 6¢　　Ⓗ 55¢

Ⓖ 16¢　　Ⓙ 61¢

3. Jose worked for Mrs. Land at her nursery for 24 hours a week last summer. How many hours did he work in 5 weeks?

Ⓐ 120 hours　　Ⓒ 168 hours

Ⓑ 140 hours　　Ⓓ 240 hours

4. Last month Ruby saw a video game that she wants to buy. The game is priced at $49.95, including tax. She has saved $28.58 so far. How much more money does Ruby need to buy the video game?

Ⓕ $78.53　　Ⓗ $21.37

Ⓖ $21.47　　Ⓙ Not given

5. Joseph and Jimmy both collect baseball cards. Joseph has 96 different cards, and Jimmy has 74. How many more cards does Joseph have than Jimmy?

Ⓐ 18　　Ⓒ 174

Ⓑ 22　　Ⓓ Not given

6. Carolina works at Louie's Pizza Shop 4 hours every day of the week during the summer. How many hours does she work each week?

Ⓕ 4　　Ⓗ 28

Ⓖ 7　　Ⓙ Not given

7. Jonathan bought a $.49 ruler, a $3.89 notebook, and a $1.10 compass with a $10 bill. If no tax was charged, how much change should he have received?

Ⓐ $5.48　　Ⓒ $4.52

Ⓑ $5.52　　Ⓓ $4.48

8. Dad's car is 14 feet long. Uncle Albert's truck is 17 feet long. What would they measure together if their bumpers were touching?
   - (F) 14 feet
   - (G) 21 feet
   - (H) 31 feet
   - (J) Not given

9. Hannah was selling programs at the game for 75¢ each. If she sold 46 programs, how much money did she take in?
   - (A) $34.00
   - (B) $34.50
   - (C) $36.50
   - (D) Not given

10. The store across the street from school only had 42 fresh doughnuts for sale. Scott bought them all and he wanted to divide them evenly among his 19 classmates by giving out only whole doughnuts. How many doughnuts did he have left over?
    - (F) 38
    - (G) 23
    - (H) 14
    - (J) 4

11. Nick has 68 Sacagawea dollars, and Robert has 42. How many more dollars would Robert need so he would have the same amount as Nick?
    - (A) 42
    - (B) 36
    - (C) 26
    - (D) 18

12. Mallery bought new socks for winter. She bought one pair for $1.98, a package of 2 pairs for $2.49, and 3 pairs for $1.29 each. How much did she pay for the 6 pairs altogether?
    - (F) $5.76
    - (G) $8.34
    - (H) $10.83
    - (J) $12.54

13. If the tax on a $14.98 CD is $1.05, how much will Kaitlin pay altogether?
    - (A) $15.95
    - (B) $15.98
    - (C) $15.03
    - (D) $16.03

14. Jamal bought 3 milkshakes and 3 chicken sandwiches for $10.50, without tax. He knew the sandwiches were $2.00 each. How much did each milkshake cost?
    - (F) $1.50
    - (G) $1.25
    - (H) $1.75
    - (J) $3.50

15. There are 960 species of insects represented at the Museum of Natural History. The fifth grade science textbook has pictures of 394 of these species. How many at the museum are not represented in the book?
    - (A) 394
    - (B) 566
    - (C) 666
    - (D) 1,354

16. The large multipurpose room has 84 chairs. Mr. Velez wants them arranged in 7 rows. How many chairs will there be in each row?
    - (F) 8
    - (G) 9
    - (H) 11
    - (J) 12

17. There are 12 popsicles in a package. Sherry and her friends ate 8 of them after school. Which fraction shows what part of the package they ate?
    - (A) $\frac{4}{8}$
    - (B) $\frac{1}{2}$
    - (C) $\frac{2}{3}$
    - (D) $\frac{3}{4}$

Percentage Correct = $\dfrac{\text{\# correct}}{\text{total \#}}$ = ___%

Grades 6–8

Problem Solving with Whole Numbers, Fractions, and Decimals

If I divide 272 by 2, then ...

Choose the correct answer for each problem.

1. The spring field trip is coming up and 493 students plan to go. At lunch time there will be a picnic. The county park has a number of areas that each have table seating for 75. How many areas should the school reserve?
- Ⓐ 6
- Ⓒ 49
- Ⓑ 7
- Ⓓ 75

2. The kennel down the street from Eric has room for 28 dogs. All the pens were full last Friday, with three fourths of them containing full-grown dogs. How many puppies were at the kennel Friday?
- Ⓕ 28
- Ⓗ 14
- Ⓖ 21
- Ⓙ 7

3. Sarah walked 3.7 miles Tuesday and 4.6 miles Wednesday. How much further did she walk on Wednesday than on Tuesday?
- Ⓐ 0.9 miles
- Ⓒ 8.3 miles
- Ⓑ 1.1 miles
- Ⓓ Not given

4. Mattie bought a frozen pizza that was marked "$5.95" at the grocery store. At the register, she used a coupon for $.38 off the purchase of one pizza. How much did she pay for the pizza, not including tax?
- Ⓕ $6.33
- Ⓗ $5.57
- Ⓖ $5.67
- Ⓙ $4.67

5. There was surprisingly little snow in March. The first week there was 1.5 inches, the second week there was 2.3 inches, the third week there was no snow, and in the fourth week 4.7 inches fell. How much snow fell in the month of March?
- Ⓐ 3.8 inches
- Ⓒ 8.5 inches
- Ⓑ 7.0 inches
- Ⓓ Not given

6. Michael worked 32 hours last week. His paycheck was for $168.00. How much did he make per hour?
- Ⓕ $10.00
- Ⓗ $3.20
- Ⓖ $5.25
- Ⓙ $1.68

7. The cookie store at the mall is featuring Chewy Chocolate Chip flavor. The first dozen cost $4.25 and then each additional cookie is $.35. If Opal needs to buy 20 cookies for her class, how much will it cost her?
- Ⓐ $10.50
- Ⓒ $10.05
- Ⓑ $7.05
- Ⓓ $8.50

8. Five friends went out Friday night to celebrate the end of the school year. They agreed to share the cost of the evening equally. Their restaurant bill for food and beverages was $38.96, and they added a $6 tip for the waiter. After dinner they played a round of miniature golf, and the total fee was $18.29. How much did each friend need to pay to cover the evening?

(F) $9.50   (H) $39.00
(G) $14.50   (J) $12.65

9. Jeff and Victor went to a concert in a neighboring city. To get there they drove 2 hours at 65 miles per hour and 30 minutes at 50 miles per hour. How many miles did they drive to get to the concert?

(A) 50   (C) 130
(B) 65   (D) 155

10. Mrs. Lawson ordered a large cake to take to her class to celebrate the anniversary of the first man on the moon. At the celebration, the class ate two-thirds of the cake. After school, Mrs. Lawson decided to take half of what was left over home to her family and leave the rest in the teachers' lounge refrigerator. How much of the cake did Mrs. Lawson take home?

(F) $\frac{1}{3}$ (H) $\frac{1}{5}$
(G) $\frac{1}{4}$ (J) $\frac{1}{6}$

11. Leona bought a new oar for her boat for $18.95 and a new life preserver for $27.99. She had saved three $20 bills to pay for the items, and her dad said he would pay for the tax. How much change did Leona get back?

(A) $24.99   (C) $13.95
(B) $23.00   (D) $13.06

12. The eighth graders in Mr. Achebe's social studies class are learning about economics. To begin the unit they read about a club that sold tickets to a variety show for $5 each. The total cost to produce the show was $248. What is the smallest number of tickets the club would need to sell to make a profit of at least $100?

(F) 70   (H) 500
(G) 95   (J) 1240

13. When Isobel's mom said she could redecorate her room, the first thing she did was go to the fabric store to choose material for new curtains. She found exactly what she wanted for $3.98 a yard. She needs 5 yards to make the curtains she has always wanted, and she decided to buy an extra yard and a half to cover a table by her bed. Without considering tax, how much will the fabric cost?

(A) $19.90   (C) $25.87
(B) $23.88   (D) $39.80

Computation and Problem Solving with Percent

*t*he word *percent* comes from the Latin *per centum*, meaning "for a hundred." We usually refer to percent as "out of a hundred" or "per hundred." Even the symbol for percent (%) looks like one hundred! From discounts to interest rates to test scores, percentages abound in our everyday lives, and a solid understanding of this concept is essential.

Standardized tests appear to have very few references to percent in grades 4 and 5, with only Illinois, Massachusetts, and New York including problems. This book does not include practice problems with percent specifically for grades 4 and 5. However, in grades 6–8, percent problems are plentiful and come in a variety of formats.

TEACHING TIPS

1. Show students that the percent symbol (%) actually looks like 100, to help them remember the meaning of percent.

2. Remind students that all of something, or one whole, is 100%. Therefore, a percent of less than 100 indicates less than all, and a percent greater than 100 means there is more than one whole.

3. Demonstrate how easily decimal numbers can be changed to percents by simply moving the decimal point two places to the right and adding the % symbol.

4. Explain that fractions can be changed to percents simply by setting up a proportion using the fraction as one ratio and 100 as the denominator of the other.

5. Present problems that involve the whole, a part, and a percent rate. Show the three basic places and how they may be missing. For instance, 20% of 80 is 16. Now write three problems:

16 is what percent of 80? 20% of 80 is what number? 16 is 20% of what number? The basic formula to solve each problem is: $\frac{Part}{Whole} = \frac{rate}{100}$.

Using this formula simplifies the teaching and learning of percent. Use it regularly, post it on the wall, and give students lots of practice solving for the missing piece using the proportion.

SUPER SUCCESS STRATEGIES

Percent

1. Remember that % *refers to 100.*

2. 1 = 100%. If you have *less than 1 whole,* then your percent will be *less than 100.*

3. If you have *more than 1 whole,* then your percent will be *greater than 100.* For instance, if you earn 150% of what you made the previous month, you made $1\frac{1}{2}$ times as much!

4. Use the basic formula $\frac{Part}{Whole} = \frac{rate}{100}$ to solve almost any problem involving percent.

5. A *decimal number can be easily changed to a percent* because a number written to the hundredth place is the same as a percent. For instance, .25 is twenty-five hundredths. That's the same as 25% because percent means "out of a hundred." A number with only tenths like .3 is the same as 30% because zero can be put in the hundredths place without changing the place value. The number .462 is 46.2%.

6. A fraction can be changed to a percent by *setting up a proportion.* Use the fraction as a ratio. The other ratio will have the unknown in the numerator and 100 in the denominator. For instance, $\frac{3}{4} = \frac{x}{100}$. By using cross products, $4x = 300$. So $x = 75$. This means that $\frac{3}{4} = 75\%$.

Computation and Problem Solving with Percent (6–8)

Test	(pages 40–41) 1	2	3	4	5	6	7	8	9	10	11	12	13	14	15	16	17	18	(page 42) 1	2	3	4
CAT			X																			
IOWA					X		X		X													
MAT7	X	X		X				X		X												
SAT9																						
Terra													X		X		X					
FCAT								X									X					
GEPA													X	X					X			
ISAT																X	X					X
LEAP												X					X					
MCAS											X									X	X	
MEAP																			X			
NYS						X											X					
PACT											X	X		X		X	X					
TAAS																		X	X			

Grades 6–8

Computation and Problem Solving with Percent

$\frac{1}{4}$ = .25

Choose the correct answer for each problem.

1. Which number is 114% of 40?
- Ⓐ 15
- Ⓒ 40
- Ⓑ 150
- Ⓓ Not given

2. What percent of 380 is 57?
- Ⓕ 38%
- Ⓗ 15%
- Ⓖ 57%
- Ⓙ Not given

3. 35% of 40 =
- Ⓐ 39
- Ⓒ 14
- Ⓑ 31
- Ⓓ 3.5

4. 28 is 80% of what number?
- Ⓕ 28
- Ⓗ 52
- Ⓖ 35
- Ⓙ Not given

5. The closest estimate of 55% of $119 is _____.
- Ⓐ $55
- Ⓒ $100
- Ⓑ $60
- Ⓓ $110

6. How is $\frac{7}{8}$ written as a percent?
- Ⓕ 87.5%
- Ⓗ 70%
- Ⓖ .875%
- Ⓙ .70%

7. Which is <u>not</u> a way to write $\frac{1}{5}$?
- Ⓐ .20%
- Ⓒ $\frac{20}{100}$
- Ⓑ .20
- Ⓓ 20%

8. How is 64% written as a fraction in simplest form?
- Ⓕ $\frac{64}{1}$
- Ⓗ $\frac{32}{50}$
- Ⓖ $\frac{64}{100}$
- Ⓙ $\frac{16}{25}$

9. This figure is a rectangle divided into 12 equal squares. If the shaded squares are taken away, what percent of the original area of the rectangle is left?

- Ⓐ 30%
- Ⓒ 75%
- Ⓑ 25%
- Ⓓ 50%

10. What percent of this figure is shaded?

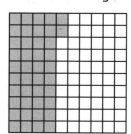

- Ⓕ .42%
- Ⓗ 0.42%
- Ⓖ 4.2%
- Ⓙ 42%

11. Jessie decided to pay for dinner Tuesday night for herself and four friends. The bill was $39.90. What is the closest amount to the tip she will leave if she leaves 15%?

(A) $6   (C) $4

(B) $5   (D) $3

12. Marissa saw in a newspaper that a computer she wants is reduced 30% for a sale. The original price is $740. What is the sale price?

(F) $710   (H) $518

(G) $770   (J) $310

13. Malcolm bought a new jacket for $39.99. The sales tax rate is 7%. About how much was the sales tax?

(A) $3.99   (C) $2.80

(B) $4.00   (D) $0.70

14. Jim earns $600 per week working as a carpenter during the summer. His employers take 7% out of each worker's salary to supply drinks, snacks, and lunch for the crew. How much of his salary does Jim keep each week?

(F) $530   (H) $420

(G) $593   (J) $558

15. Latisha's mom took Latisha and her friends out for pizza. One of the girls had some money from a part-time job and wanted to leave a 15% tip for the waiter. How much did she leave as a tip if the total bill was $28?

(A) $15.00   (C) $1.30

(B) $2.80   (D) $4.20

16. Jay has his eye on a $300 surfboard. He waits to buy it until it is reduced 15%. What is the sale price of the board?

(F) $45   (H) $285

(G) $255   (J) $215

17. Tony purchased a guitar song book on sale that had an original price of $15.00. All of the guitar books were marked 20% off. He also had to pay 8% sales tax. What was the total price Tony paid, in dollars and cents?

(A) $12.00   (C) $13.20

(B) $12.96   (D) $16.20

18. The circle graph shows the eye colors of the students in Mrs. Brantley's class. About what percent of the class have green eyes?

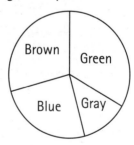

(F) 20%   (H) 45%

(G) 30%   (J) 50%

Grades 6–8

Computation and Problem Solving with Percent

25% of 16 is . . .

Choose the correct answer for each problem.

1. Three hundred twenty students were asked to name their favorite Harry Potter book. The results are shown on the circle graph. What was the total number of students who named Book III or Book IV as their favorite?

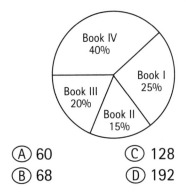

Book IV 40%

Book I 25%

Book III 20%

Book II 15%

Ⓐ 60   Ⓒ 128
Ⓑ 68   Ⓓ 192

2. Book sales during the fall book fair are shown on the chart. About what percent of all of the books sold at the fair were sold through orders on Wednesday?

Purchases	Monday	Tuesday	Wednesday	Thursday	Friday
Cash	29	38	32	37	76
Orders	21	47	54	61	85

Ⓕ .54%   Ⓗ 18%
Ⓖ 11%   Ⓙ 54%

3. There are 4 main rooms in the front wing of Harris Middle School. The square footage of each is listed on the chart. About what percentage of the total square footage of the front wing is the area of the counseling center?

Room	Square footage
Reception area	164
Counseling center	280
Computer lab	410
Teacher lounge	350

Ⓐ 10%   Ⓒ 35%
Ⓑ 25%   Ⓓ 45%

4. The chart shows the ice cream flavor preferences of the 7th grade. What percent of the total class prefers chocolate?

FLAVOR	STUDENTS (each • = 10 students)
Vanilla	• • • •
Cherry	• • • • • •
Chocolate	• • • • • • • • • • • • • • •

Ⓕ 60%   Ⓗ 140%
Ⓖ 14%   Ⓙ 50%

Ratio and Proportion

*r*atio and proportion should not be mysteries to students. The concepts can be taught right along with fractions. In fact, referring to fractions as ratios will make students more comfortable with proportions, which are nothing more than equivalent fractions. Standardized tests in grades 4 and 5 do not deal with ratio and proportion concepts to any great extent, yet tests in grades 6, 7, and 8 do, and they also apply these concepts in problem-solving items.

TEACHING TIPS

1. Explain that a ratio is simply a comparison.

2. Show the ways a ratio may be expressed:

2 to 3 $\qquad$ 2 : 3 $\qquad$ $\frac{2}{3}$

3. After doing many examples of ratios with students, tell them that two equivalent ratios form a proportion.

4. Emphasize the relationships among the numerators and denominators in a proportion. Teach students the concept of "cross products." For instance, if $\frac{3}{4} = \frac{15}{20}$, then $3 \times 20 = 4 \times 15$.

5. Show students that proportion allows us to solve for unknowns. For instance, if we know that $\frac{2}{3} = \frac{x}{12}$, then we can use "cross products" to solve for x. We know that $24 = 3x$, so $x = 8$. This is algebra!

6. Have students practice writing proportions with the unknown (variable) in different positions. Then have them solve for the unknown.

Ratio and Proportion

1. Before trying to find a missing value, make sure your *ratios are set up right.*

2. *Look at units*—they must be the same for numerators and the same for denominators.

3. *Units must match!* If time is in the numerator, don't compare minutes to hours. Change hours to minutes before beginning to solve. If length is in the denominator, don't compare inches to feet. Change feet to inches.

4. *"Cross products"* are equal in proportions. Use this fact to find values of unknowns.

Ratio and Proportion (4–5)

	page 45				
Test	1	2	3	4	5
CAT		X			
MAT7	X				
ISAT					X
PACT			X	X	
TAAS			X		

Ratio and Proportion (6–8)

	page 46–47														
Test	1	2	3	4	5	6	7	8	9	10	11	12	13	14	15
CAT						X									
IOWA		X										X		X	
MAT7									X	X			X	X	X
FCAT					X								X		
GEPA		X													
ISAT			X				X	X					X		X
LEAP			X	X											X
MEAP			X	X				X	X				X		X
NYS	X						X							X	
PACT	X		X				X	X			X		X	X	X
TASS	X						X							X	

Ratio and Proportion

1:3, 2:6 …

Choose the correct answer to each problem.

1. In the baseball toss game, Romero threw 1 out of 3 balls through the target. If he continues to do this well, how many throws could he expect to make out of 24 tries?

   Ⓐ 12   Ⓑ 8   Ⓒ 18   Ⓓ 10

2. Chelsea's bead collection includes 8 blue, 14 yellow, and 22 green. What is the ratio of blue beads to green beads?

   Ⓕ 8 to 22   Ⓖ 22 to 8   Ⓗ 8 to 44   Ⓙ 44 to 22

3. It takes Hannah 8 minutes to walk home. Her younger brother takes 10 minutes to walk the same distance. Their mom kept track of a certain number of trips and said that Hannah had walked a total of 40 minutes. If her brother walked the same amount of trips home, how long did he walk?

   Ⓐ 80 minutes Ⓑ 50 minutes Ⓒ 48 minutes Ⓓ 32 minutes

4. Willa's recipe for 2 dozen chocolate chip cookies calls for 3 cups of flour. She wants to make three dozen cookies. How much flour will she need?

   Ⓕ $7\frac{1}{4}$ Ⓖ 5   Ⓗ $4\frac{1}{2}$ Ⓙ 3

5. Four out of five students in the fifth grade say their favorite pizza has pepperoni as one of the toppings. If there are 80 students in the fifth grade, how many of them prefer pepperoni on their pizza?

   Ⓐ 16   Ⓑ 45   Ⓒ 64   Ⓓ 76

Grades 6–8

Ratio and Proportion

The cross product is . . .

Choose the correct answer for each problem.

1. If $\frac{x}{32} = \frac{3}{8}$, what is the value of x?

  Ⓐ 10   Ⓒ 14

  Ⓑ 12   Ⓓ 16

2. There were 12 new trucks brought to the sales lot Monday. Three of them were red. At this rate, if 40 trucks are brought to the lot by Thursday, how many of them will be red?

  Ⓕ 10   Ⓗ 15

  Ⓖ 12   Ⓙ 16

3. At the end of the school year Mark dumped out the contents of his book bag. He found 4 colors of markers— 6 black, 3 red, 5 blue, and 2 green. What is the ratio of black markers to green markers?

  Ⓐ 1 to 3   Ⓒ 6 to 16

  Ⓑ 6 to 5   Ⓓ 3 to 1

4. In her cooperative group of 5, Jasmine knows she needs 20 sets of cards to play a game. If she teaches the whole class of 19 students to play the game, how many sets of cards will she need?

  Ⓕ 20   Ⓗ 39

  Ⓖ 25   Ⓙ 76

5. Four pairs of socks cost $5.00. How much would 2 dozen pairs of socks cost?

  Ⓐ $10.00   Ⓒ $30.00

  Ⓑ $24.00   Ⓓ $120.00

6. Corky rides his bike almost every afternoon. On one course he rides for speed for a set period of time. If he rides 12 miles in 25 minutes, which formula could he use to figure out how far he could ride in an hour at this rate?

  Ⓕ $\frac{12}{25} = \frac{m}{60}$ Ⓗ $\frac{12}{25} = \frac{1}{m}$

  Ⓖ $\frac{12}{25} = \frac{60}{m}$ Ⓙ $\frac{60}{25} = \frac{12}{m}$

7. Sarah bought 12 pounds of fresh peaches she picked for $8.50. Her mom asked her to go back the next day and pick 20 pounds. How much will the 20 pounds cost?

  Ⓐ $12.00   Ⓒ $20.50

  Ⓑ $14.17   Ⓓ $28.00

8. During the school year, Mrs. Markle's language arts class read 352 books. Of these, 220 were fiction. What was the ratio of nonfiction to fiction books?

   F $\frac{9}{23}$ H $\frac{5}{8}$

   G $\frac{15}{23}$ J $\frac{3}{5}$

9. Jeremiah uses 8 eggs to make omelets to serve 3 friends. How many eggs would he need if his 3 friends each brought 2 guests?

   A 24 eggs   C 18 eggs

   B 16 eggs   D 12 eggs

10. How many foot-long portions could James cut from a 3-yard giant submarine sandwich?

   F 3   H 12

   G 36   J 9

11. For delivering flyers Grant is paid $72 every 3 days. If he delivers flyers 5 days in a row, how much will he be paid for those days?

   A $360   C $120

   B $144   D $80

12. 25 of the 30 students in Mr. Edward's 7th grade science class plan to take biology in high school. Use these numbers to predict how many of the 420 7th graders at JFK Middle School plan to take biology?

   F 300   H 350

   G 354   J 390

13. The Rivers Middle School library has 800 fiction books and 1200 nonfiction books. What is the ratio of fiction to nonfiction books?

   A $\frac{2}{3}$ C $\frac{3}{2}$

   B $\frac{1}{3}$ D $\frac{400}{800}$

14. If $\frac{5}{6} = \frac{c}{42}$, what is the value of c?

   F 20   H 30

   G 25   J 35

15. Cleopha cleaned out her sock drawer. She discovered that she had 5 pairs of white socks, 3 pairs of navy socks, 4 pairs of black socks and 12 pairs in a variety of colors. What is the ratio of navy socks to black socks?

   A 3 to 5   C 3 to 4

   B 3 to 12   D 4 to 12

Expanded and Scientific Notation

*e*xpanded notation calls for knowledge of place value. It is rarely tested in grades 4 and 5. When it is, students are asked to write a number in expanded form through the thousands place value. In grades 6–8 students are asked to not only use expanded notation, but also to apply the concept of scientific notation, which allows students to deal with very large and very small numbers in reasonable ways.

TEACHING TIPS

1. Give lots of practice converting numbers in standard form to expanded form, emphasizing place value.

2. Show students how to work with powers of 10 so they can convert regular expanded notation to expanded notation with exponents.

3. Work with students' science teachers to teach scientific notation in the context of science concepts.

4. Provide many examples of why scientific notation plays a role in the real world with very large numbers, commonly used in astronomy, and very small numbers, commonly used in chemistry and biology.

Expanded and Scientific Notation

1. Expanded notation includes *taking a number apart*, digit by digit, and putting the right number of zeroes with each. For instance, 246 is 200 + 40 + 6.

2. When you are given a number in expanded notation, *put as many blanks on your paper* as the largest place value and then *fill in the blanks*. For instance, 5,000,000 + 400,000 + 3,000 + 800 + 9 = 5 4 _ 3 8 _ 9 . Then put zeroes in the blanks without digits and add commas to make 5,403,809.

3. When a positive exponent is used in scientific notation, move the decimal to the right to create a larger number. When a negative exponent is used, move the decimal to the left to create a smaller number. The power of 10 tells us how many places the decimal must be moved. For example, $2.3706 \times 10^6 = 2,370,600$ and $1.283 \times 10^{-5} = 0.00001283$.

4. *Practice using all the rules* for both expanded and scientific notation.

5. Read each item carefully to make sure you *understand what you are being asked to do.*

Expanded and Scientific Notation (6–8)

	page 50							
Test	1	2	3	4	5	6	7	8
CAT								X
IOWA	X	X			X	X		
MAT7		X		X		X	X	
SAT9	X	X		X	X	X	X	
Terra								
FCAT			X		X		X	
GEPA			X					
MCAS			X			X		
NYS								

Grades 6–8

Expanded and Scientific Notation

If the exponent is negative, then...

Choose the correct answer for each problem.

1. What is another way to write 6,480,000?

(A) 648×10^3 (B) 64.8×10^4 (C) 6.48×10^4 (D) 6.48×10^6

2. What is the standard form of 6,000,000 + 300 + 2?

(F) 60,320   (G) 603,020   (H) 6,000,032   (J) 6,000,302

3. What is 3,420.7 written in scientific notation?

(A) 3.4207×10^3 (B) 34.207×10^2 (C) 0.34207×10^4 (D) 0.34207×10^5

4. 70,070 =

(F) 70,000 + 700   (G) 700,000 + 7   (H) 7,000,000 + 7   (J) 70,000 + 70

5. What is another way to write 1.79×10^7?

(A) 179,000,000   (B) 17,900,000   (C) 1,790,000,000   (D) 1,790,000

6. What is another way to write 4609?

(F) 4000 + 600 + 90   (H) 4000 + 600 + 9

(G) 400 + 60 + 9   (J) 4000 + 60 + 9

7. Which number is equivalent to (4 x 100,000) + (6 x 10,000) + (3 x 100) + (9 x 1)?

(A) 4609   (B) 463,009   (C) 460,039   (D) 460,309

8. What is another way to write 4,000,000 + 50,000 + 6000 + 300 + 7?

(F) 4,056,037   (G) 4,506,307   (H) 4,056,307   (J) 4,056,370

Multiples and Factors

*t*he concepts of multiple and factor can be confusing for students. While these ideas are integral to many operations in elementary math, they are often taught in isolation so students don't see that multiples and factors are really a part of concepts they already understand. Ideally, multiples should be taught along with writing equivalent fractions, since using multiples helps students find common denominators. Similarly, factors should be taught along with multiplication and division; using the terminology in the context of these basic operations makes it easier for students to use prime factorization to determine least common multiples and greatest common factors.

TEACHING TIPS

1. Show how multiples and factors are used in everyday operations, such as multiplication and division.

2. Remind students that the word *multiple* means we are multiplying, so multiples get bigger.

3. When teaching multiplication, refer to the numbers being multiplied as factors.

4. Habitually ask students to identify numbers as prime or composite, rather than teaching prime numbers as an isolated concept.

Multiples and Factors

1. *"Multiple" sounds like multiply.* That's what we do to get multiples! They are equal to or bigger than the number itself.

2. A *common multiple* of two numbers is always their product, but it's not always the *least common multiple*. For instance, a common multiple of 3 and 6 is their product 18. But the least common multiple is 6 itself because both 3 and 6 divide into it without remainders.

3. *Factors are simply numbers that divide evenly into another number.* For instance, the factors of 12 are the numbers that divide evenly into it: 1, 2, 3, 4, 6, and 12.

4. *Prime numbers* are numbers that have only two factors, themselves and 1. *Prime factors* are prime numbers that divide evenly into a number. For instance, the prime factors of the number 12 are 2 and 3.

5. *Prime factorization* means that we find the prime numbers that give the product of a number. For instance, the prime factorization of 12 is $2 \times 2 \times 3$.

6. *Know the difference* between factors and prime factors. Watch for the word *prime*.

7. *Read word problems carefully* to decide if you need to find multiples and/or factors.

Multiples and Factors (4–5)

Test	pages 54–55														
	1	2	3	4	5	6	7	8	9	10	11	12	13	14	15
CAT					X	X									
IOWA															
MAT7	X	X	X	X								X	X		X
SAT9									X						
Terra		X									X		X		
FCAT															
ESPA															
ISAT															
LEAP										X					
MCAS															
MEAP										X					
NYS		X					X						X	X	
PACT	X	X		X			X					X		X	X
TAAS								X							

Multiples and Factors (6–8)

Test	pages 56–57														
	1	2	3	4	5	6	7	8	9	10	11	12	13	14	15
CAT									X						X
IOWA															
MAT7			X	X			X	X							
SAT9	X														
Terra															
FCAT										X					
GEPA		X									X				
ISAT															
LEAP															
MCAS					X		X						X		
MEAP															
NYS						X					X	X		X	
PACT													X		X
TAAS							X			X					

Grades 4–5

Multiples and Factors

A prime factor of 27 is . . .

Choose the correct answer to each problem.

1. Allison made cookies for her class. She put the cookies in 4 equal groups with none left over. How many cookies could Allison have made?

   Ⓐ 42   Ⓒ 50
   Ⓑ 46   Ⓓ 52

2. There are 4 floors in a downtown parking garage. If equal numbers of cars are parked on each floor and there are 96 cars altogether, how many cars are there on each floor?

   Ⓕ 24   Ⓗ 92
   Ⓖ 42   Ⓙ Not given

3. The entire fifth grade was going on a picnic. The lunchroom staff baked special cookies for the day. They put 750 cookies into 150 bags, each with the same number of cookies. How many cookies did they put in each bag?

   Ⓐ 4   Ⓒ 6
   Ⓑ 5   Ⓓ Not given

4. Which shows 30 as the product of prime factors?

   Ⓕ 15 x 2   Ⓗ 3 x 10
   Ⓖ 2 x 3 x 5   Ⓙ 1 x 30

5. Which sentence is true about multiples?

   Ⓐ Multiples of 4 are always even numbers.
   Ⓑ Multiples of 5 are always odd numbers.
   Ⓒ Multiples of 6 are sometimes odd and sometimes even.
   Ⓓ Multiples of 7 are always odd.

6. Which number is a common factor of 14 and 49?

   Ⓕ 49   Ⓗ 7
   Ⓖ 14   Ⓙ 3

7. What is the greatest common factor of 20 and 35?

   Ⓐ 4   Ⓒ 7
   Ⓑ 5   Ⓓ 10

8. Which answer choice is equal to 72?

   Ⓕ 2 x 3 x 7
   Ⓖ 2 x 2 x 3 x 3
   Ⓗ 2 x 2 x 2 x 3 x 3
   Ⓙ 2 x 2 x 3 x 3 x 3

9. Ashley has an idea for a game that will require the same number of boys and girls on each team. Her afterschool program has 36 boys and 24 girls. What is the largest number of teams Ashley could form?
   (A) 2   (C) 5
   (B) 4   (D) 12

10. Eddie has collected baseball cards that are duplicates of the ones he wants to keep. If he wants to divide the duplicates equally among 4 friends, how many cards does he have to give away?
    (F) 26   (H) 30
    (G) 28   (J) 34

11. In a math game Mike's group is asked to find an even multiple of 7 that is greater than 40 and less than 53. What should the group answer?
    (A) 14   (C) 42
    (B) 28   (D) 49

12. Which shows 42 as the product of prime factors?
    (F) 3 x 14   (H) 6 x 7
    (G) 2 x 3 x 7 (J) 1 x 42

13. Shanese has 6 shelves of Beanie Babies in her room. If 72 are divided evenly among the shelves, how many are on each shelf?
    (A) 12   (C) 24
    (B) 16   (D) Not given

14. Which number is NOT a common factor of 12 and 16?
    (F) 1   (H) 3
    (G) 2   (J) 4

15. For Maria's birthday her mother wants to give the students in the fifth grade class a taste of Mexico where Maria's family lived until a year ago. She wants to take enough sopapillas for each student to have 3. Which is a number she should NOT take?
    (A) 42   (C) 51
    (B) 48   (D) 65

Grades 6–8

Multiples and Factors

A common multiple of 16 and 20 is…

Choose the correct answer for each problem.

1. Here is a factor tree. Choose the numbers that are missing from the tree.

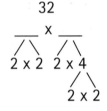

32

___ x ___

2 x 2   2 x 4

2 x 2

Ⓐ 2, 4   Ⓒ 4, 8
Ⓑ 2, 16   Ⓓ 8, 8

2. Choose the statement that is true about the numbers 14 and 42.
Ⓕ They are both factors of 24.
Ⓖ 14 is the greatest common factor.
Ⓗ They are prime numbers.
Ⓙ They are powers of 4

3. What is the fewest number of chocolate chip cookies that can be shared equally among 6 cooperative learning groups with none left over, or among 15 individual students with none left over?
Ⓐ 30   Ⓒ 15
Ⓑ 90   Ⓓ 21

4. Elijah brought licorice to share with friends. He has 42 pieces of black licorice and 36 pieces of cherry licorice. If he wants to give each friend equal amounts of black and cherry, what is the greatest number of friends with whom he could share the candy and not have any left over?
Ⓕ 12   Ⓗ 2
Ⓖ 6   Ⓙ 4

5. Stephanie is playing a number game in math. She tells her class that she is thinking of a number that is a factor of both 28 and 70. What is the biggest number she could be thinking of?
Ⓐ 2   Ⓒ 14
Ⓑ 7   Ⓓ 28

6. What is the prime factor configuration of 72?
Ⓕ 7^2 Ⓗ 8 x 9
Ⓖ 2 x 2 x 2 x 3 x 3   Ⓙ 2 x 2 x 2 x 9

7. Which expression shows 36 as the product of prime factors?
   - (A) 2 x 18
   - (B) 2 x 2 x 9
   - (C) 4 x 3 x 3
   - (D) 2 x 2 x 3 x 3

8. Choose another way to express 2 x 2 x 3 x 3 x 3 x 2 x 2.
   - (F) 4^2 x 3^3 x 1^4
   - (G) 23 x 34
   - (H) 2^2 x 3^3 x 4
   - (J) 2^2 x 3^3

9. Which of these numbers is a common multiple of 2, 3, and 7?
   - (A) 14
   - (B) 21
   - (C) 35
   - (D) 42

10. Which expression is equivalent to 3^4?
    - (F) 4 x 4 x 4
    - (G) 4 x 4
    - (H) 3 x 3 x 3 x 3
    - (J) 3 x 3 x 3

11. Which number equals 6^3?
    - (A) 18
    - (B) 36
    - (C) 63
    - (D) 216

12. Which number is prime?
    - (F) 1
    - (G) 21
    - (H) 51
    - (J) 61

13. What is the least common multiple of 5 and 7?
    - (A) 70
    - (B) 35
    - (C) 20
    - (D) 12

14. What is the least common multiple of 3, 8, and 9?
    - (F) 9
    - (G) 24
    - (H) 27
    - (J) 72

15. What is the least common multiple of 18 and 8?
    - (A) 2
    - (B) 4
    - (C) 26
    - (D) 72

Estimation and Rounding

*e*stimation is a valuable life tool. Deciding how much money to bring along when we go out to the movies, figuring out the cost of an item marked down 30%, determining the time it will take to run our errands—most of the mathematical situations in our everyday lives can be answered through estimation rather than requiring exact calculation. The skill of estimation is often difficult to assess for two reasons: there is no exact answer in open-ended settings and we cannot tell if a student found the exact answer and then chose a good estimate. Yet we should not let the difficulty in effectively assessing estimation skills keep us from emphasizing estimation as an important math tool.

Rounding is a skill that allows us to make meaningful estimations. The rules that govern rounding are straightforward. We need to give many opportunities to practice both rounding and estimation.

TEACHING TIPS

1. Display examples of rounding to various place values. Ask students to round often.

2. Give a variety of opportunities for students to estimate, from how many marbles are in a jar to the distance from the classroom door to the stairway. This mental exercise is excellent practice.

3. Show students the relationship between rounding and estimation.

4. Discuss the appropriate use of estimation, along with how to recognize when exact computation is needed.

Estimation and Rounding

1. Rounding is a type of estimation! *Pay attention to the place value* to which you are asked to round. For instance, rounding 673 to the tens position would be 670 and to the hundreds position would be 700.

2. In problems, watch out for the words *"about," "estimate," "close to"* and *"between which numbers."*

3. Remember that estimation is something we use every day. *Practice it!*

Estimation and Rounding (4–5)

Test	pages 61–62												
	1	2	3	4	5	6	7	8	9	10	11	12	13
CAT							X	X					X
IOWA			X			X	X		X	X		X	X
MAT7	X	X	X	X	X	X							
SAT9		X	X	X	X						X		
Terra	X			X				X					
FCAT													
ESPA													
ISAT													
LEAP													
MCAS									X			X	
MEAP													
NYS						X							X
PACT									X			X	
TAAS	X								X		X	X	

Estimation and Rounding (6–8)

Test	pages 63–64															
	1	2	3	4	5	6	7	8	9	10	11	12	13	14	15	16
CAT																X
IOWA									X	X	X					
MAT7							X	X								
SAT9	X						X						X			
Terra												X				
FCAT																
GEPA				X												X
ISAT							X									
LEAP	X											X	X	X		
MCAS															X	
MEAP	X											X	X	X		
NYS																
PACT																
TAAS		X	X		X	X										

60

Grades 4–5

Estimation and Rounding

To estimate the total cost...

Choose the correct answer to each problem.

1. Jonah bought a new comb for $2.99, a pen for $1.49, and a candy bar for $0.57. About how much did he spend before tax was added?
(A) $7.00   (C) $5.00
(B) $6.00   (D) $4.00

2. If it takes Dan about 12 minutes to walk to Emily's house and back, what is the closest estimate of the time it would take for him to walk to and from her house 4 times?
(F) Between 25 and 30 minutes
(G) Between 35 and 40 minutes
(H) Between 45 and 50 minutes
(J) Between 55 and 60 minutes

3. Mrs. Stiles received 5 boxes of paperback books for the media center. Each box contained 42 books. About how many books did she receive?
(A) 200   (C) 100
(B) 150   (D) 50

4. Manuel chose a book to read during summer vacation. It had 1120 pages. What is this number rounded to the nearest hundred?
(F) 1000   (H) 1200
(G) 1100   (J) 1300

5. Yolanda reported that there is a $3,280,500 budget for her corporation. What is this number rounded to the nearest hundred thousand?
(A) $3,000,000   (C) $3,200,000
(B) $3,280,000   (D) $3,300,000

6. The closest estimate of 4162 ÷ 19 is between:
(F) 200 and 300   (H) 10 and 20
(G) 100 and 200   (J) 20 and 30

7. To *estimate* the sum of 53, 39, and 75 by rounding to the nearest tens, what numbers would you use?
(A) 50, 30, 70   (C) 55, 40, 75
(B) 50, 40, 70   (D) 50, 40, 80

8. If a number rounded to the nearest hundred is 400 and the number is more than 447, which number could it be?

   F) 446   H) 448
   G) 399   J) 450

9. Jill bought small gifts for 4 of her friends when she visited Yellowstone National Park. If the gifts cost $1.40, $2.80, $1.95 and $3.25, what is the closest *estimate* of the cost of the gifts?

   A) $7   C) $11
   B) $9   D) $13

10. The closest *estimate* of the answer to 340 ÷ 6 is _____.

    F) 6   H) 600
    G) 60   J) 6000

11. Derek reads about 20 minutes a day. *About* how many minutes does he read in 3 weeks?

    A) 140   C) 300
    B) 200   D) 400

12. ChinLee wants to buy some things he will need on his trip to the beach. In a shop he finds sunglasses for $6.98, a beach towel for $5.29, and a pair of flip flops for $8.69. What is the best estimate of how much money he'll need for his purchases?

    F) $19.00   H) $24.00
    G) $21.00   J) $25.00

13. To estimate the product of 12, 19, 23, and 37 by rounding to the nearest tens, what numbers would you use?

    A) 10, 20, 20, 40
    B) 10, 20, 20, 35
    C) 10, 20, 20, 30
    D) 10, 20, 25, 40

Grades 6–8

Estimation and Rounding

Rounding 43 to the nearest 10 …

Choose the correct answer for each problem.

1. Rebecca wants to have $800 in her savings account by August 1. By June 1, she had $269 and by July 4, she had $318 more. What is the best *estimate* of how much she still needs to earn to make her goal?

  Ⓐ $100   Ⓒ $300
  Ⓑ $200   Ⓓ $400

2. Six friends went to the movies Saturday. The tickets cost $4.95 each. They parked their van in the parking garage for $6.00. What is the best *estimate* of the total amount they spent?

  Ⓕ $11   Ⓗ $36
  Ⓖ $30   Ⓙ $40

3. Ricardo needs to buy 9 concert tickets. Altogether, he and his friends have $120 to spend. Ricardo said he would go to the ticket office and buy the best seats he can get for this amount. What is the best *estimate* of the ticket price he will be able to purchase?

  Ⓐ $12   Ⓒ $20
  Ⓑ $16   Ⓓ $25

4. What is the best *estimate* for the weight of a math text book?

  Ⓕ 3 pounds   Ⓗ 6 grams
  Ⓖ 8 ounces   Ⓙ 10 liters

5. The cost of one game of bowling is $1.90. If 10 students each bowl one game, what is the best *estimate* of the cost?

  Ⓐ $15.00   Ⓒ $25.00
  Ⓑ $20.00   Ⓓ $30.00

6. Joelle jogs 3 to 5 miles each day. A *reasonable* estimate of the total distance Joelle jogs in a week is ____.

  Ⓕ 5 miles   Ⓗ 28 miles
  Ⓖ 18 miles   Ⓙ 40 miles

7. Shawna found a skirt she wanted on sale for $19.50. Her friend said the original price when summer started was $35.95. Choose the best *estimate* of the difference between the sale price and the original price.

  Ⓐ $10.00   Ⓒ $45.00
  Ⓑ $15.00   Ⓓ $50.00

8. Noah wants to go bungee jumping with his friend Austin. If his mom says he can do it, Noah will need to save $75 by the end of the summer. If he mows 4 lawns a week at $20 a lawn and saves half, *about* how many weeks will it take to save enough money to pay for a bungee-jumping experience?

    F) 1 week   H) 3 weeks
    G) 2 weeks   J) 4 weeks

9. The closest *estimate* to the actual cost of one balloon is _____ if they are 4 for $8.50.

    A) more than $2.50
    B) between $2.20 and $2.50
    C) between $2.00 and $2.20
    D) less than $2.00

10. The closest *estimate* of 4.52 − 1.09 is between _____.

    F) 1.50 and 2.00
    G) 2.00 and 2.50
    H) 2.50 and 3.00
    J) 3.00 and 3.50

11. The closest *estimate* of $6\frac{5}{7}$ x $4\frac{1}{9}$ is

    _____.

    A) 24   C) 46
    B) 28   D) 64

12. What is the best *estimate* of 0.2 x 40.8?

    F) 8   H) 10
    G) 9   J) 16

13. If 38.64819 is rounded to 38.648, then it is rounded to the nearest

    _____.

    A) tenth
    B) hundredth
    C) thousandth
    D) hundred thousandth

14. If 862,841 and 659,088 are each rounded to the nearest ten thousand, what will the difference be between the two numbers?

    F) 20,000   H) 1,520,000
    G) 200,000   J) 152,000

15. Brian drove 138 miles on the 8.5 gallons of gas he put in his tank after he ran out of gas last week. About how many miles per gallon did he average, rounded to the nearest mile?

    A) 8.5   C) 17
    B) 16   D) 18

16. How many of the following numbers could be 1,847,000 when rounded to the nearest thousand?

    1,847,299
    1,847,009
    1,846,900
    1,846,503

    F) 0   H) 3
    G) 2   J) 4

Order of Operations

*t*he rules for order of operations were established to create international consistency when a problem requires performing more than one operation. These rules are built into calculators as algebraic logic. They should become a natural part of how our students approach mathematics.

Standardized tests rarely ask fourth and fifth graders to use the rules of order of operations. Sixth, seventh, and eighth graders are asked in some tests to use the rules in very straightforward ways. The questions require only the four basic operations and not the use of parentheses or exponents.

TEACHING TIPS

1. Teach the rules of order of operations using some catchy device such as the phrase known by millions—Please Excuse My Dear Aunt Sally (parentheses, exponents, multiplication, division, addition, subtraction).

2. Show students what a difference the use of the order of operations rules make in solving equations. For instance, if you solve $6 + 4 \times 2 - 3$ by simply working left to right, the answer is 17. However, using order of operations, the answer is 11.

3. Give many opportunities to practice using the order of operations rules.

Order of Operations

There's a saying that many students use to remember the rules of order of operations: Please Excuse My Dear Aunt Sally. Generations of students have remembered the rules this way. Here's what PEMDAS means in math terms.

P —do everything within parentheses first

E —next take care of exponents

M
D ⎤—do all multiplication and division from left to right

A
S ⎤—do all addition and subtraction from left to right

During tests, it is a good idea to *write PEMDAS at the top of some scrap paper* as a reminder of order of operations during the exam.

Order of Operations (6–8)

	page 67				
Test	1	2	3	4	5
IOWA			X		
MAT7		X			
FCAT					X
GEPA	X				
MCAS				X	
PACT	X	X	X		

Grades 6–8

Order of Operations

PEMDAS

Choose the correct answer to each problem.

1. 6 + 15 ÷ 3 + 16 =

   Ⓐ 21   Ⓑ 23   Ⓒ 27   Ⓓ 30

2. Solve 24 – 3 x 6 ÷ 2 –1 =

   Ⓕ 21   Ⓖ 14   Ⓗ 62   Ⓙ 19

3. What is the answer to 16 ÷ 2 x 3 – 1 =

   Ⓐ 18   Ⓑ 23   Ⓒ 50   Ⓓ 51

4. What operation should be performed first in this expression?

   8 – 3 + 12 ÷ 3 x 2

   Ⓕ addition   Ⓖ subtraction   Ⓗ multiplication   Ⓙ division

5. What operation should be performed first in this expression?

   7 + $\frac{11-2}{3}$ x 4

   Ⓐ addition   Ⓑ subtraction   Ⓒ multiplication   Ⓓ division

Integers

a number is an integer if it is a whole number, the opposite of a whole number, or zero. These numbers can be effectively illustrated on a number line. Younger students are often told that we "can't take a bigger number from a smaller one." And then in fifth grade or so, integers are introduced and we tell students that now we *can* take a bigger number from a smaller one. A confusing message, to say the least! Even though integer operations are part of the curriculum of most middle-grade math classes, not all standardized tests contain integer items. Some use integers-only in algebraic equations as in Chapter 2.

TEACHING TIPS

1. Introduce integers by talking about real-world examples of negative numbers, including discussions of above and below sea level, banking credits and debits, and temperature.

2. Display a large number line in the classroom and refer to it often.

3. Teach multiplication and division of integers before addition and subtraction to build the confidence of your students.

4. Teach addition of integers after multiplication and division. When students have mastered these three operations, proceed to subtraction. Subtraction of integers is the most difficult operation to comprehend.

Integers

1. Use a *number line* to help you understand positive and negative number relationships.

2. *Multiplying and dividing* integers are easy operations! Look at the signs and don't miss the simple ones.

3. Think of *adding* integers as *putting numbers together*. For instance, when you add 2 positive numbers you get a positive number, and when you add 2 negative numbers you get a negative number. When you add negative and positive numbers, find the difference of the two numbers and the sign will be the one used with the number that is the greatest distance from zero.

4. *Change all integer subtraction problems to addition problems* by changing the subtraction sign to an addition sign. Then change the sign of the number following that sign. For instance, 6 − (-3) becomes 6 + (+3) and -7 − 4 becomes -7 + (-4).

Integers (6–8)

Test	pages 70–71																			
	1	2	3	4	5	6	7	8	9	10	11	12	13	14	15	16	17	18	19	20
CAT	X	X	X	X	X	X	X	X	X			X				X				X
IOWA											X									
MAT7										X					X					
SAT9																X				
Terra																				
FCAT																			X	
GEPA													X							
ISAT																	X			
LEAP																		X		
MCAS														X						
MEAP																		X		
NYS													X							
PACT	X	X		X		X						X								

Grades 6–8

Integers

Choose the correct answer for each problem.

5 minus a – 2 is...

1. –8 + –3 =
- (A) –11
- (B) –5
- (C) 11
- (D) None of these

2. –36 ÷ 9 =
- (F) 27
- (G) –4
- (H) 4
- (J) None of these

3. –7 + (6 + –4) =
- (A) –9
- (B) –17
- (C) –5
- (D) None of these

4. What number is the same as |–16|?
- (F) 4
- (G) –16
- (H) 16
- (J) None of these

5. What temperature is colder than –22°F?
- (A) –24°F
- (B) 0°F
- (C) –20°F
- (D) None of these

6. 20 – –4 =
- (F) –9
- (G) –17
- (H) –5
- (J) None of these

7. 20 + –3 =
- (A) 17
- (B) 23
- (C) –23
- (D) None of these

8. 14 – (8 – 3) =
- (F) 3
- (G) 9
- (H) 25
- (J) None of these

9. Which number is less than 3 and greater than –7?
- (A) 8
- (B) 4
- (C) –2
- (D) None of these

10. Which represents the greatest value?
- (F) –6 + 3
- (G) 6 – –3
- (H) –6 x 3
- (J) None of these

11. 48 ÷ –3 =
- (A) 16
- (B) 45
- (C) –16
- (D) None of these

Name _____

12. −14 − 4 =
 Ⓕ −10
 Ⓖ −18
 Ⓗ 18
 Ⓙ None of these

13. 19 − 7 − 5 =
 Ⓐ 12
 Ⓑ 14
 Ⓒ 7
 Ⓓ None of these

14. Which is the coldest temperature?
 Ⓕ −14°C
 Ⓖ −9°C
 Ⓗ 0°C
 Ⓙ None of these

15. Which arrow most accurately points to −1¾?

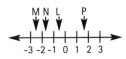

 Ⓐ M
 Ⓑ N
 Ⓒ L
 Ⓓ P

16. It was −8°C when Jenny looked at the thermometer outside her classroom during math class yesterday. If the temperature rises 20°, what will the thermometer read?
 Ⓕ −28°
 Ⓖ −12°
 Ⓗ 12°
 Ⓙ 28°

17. In which set of numbers are the integers in order from least to greatest?
 Ⓐ −8, −6, −2, 0, 2, 6
 Ⓑ 6, 2, 0, −8, −6, −2
 Ⓒ 6, 2, 0, −2, −6, −8
 Ⓓ −8, −6, 6, −2, 2, 0

18. Which set of integers is in ascending order?
 Ⓕ −9, −4, −1, 0, 2, 7
 Ⓖ −9, −1, −4, 0, 2, 7
 Ⓗ 7, 2, 0, −1, −4, −9
 Ⓙ 0, −1, 2, −4, 7, −9

19. When −4 and a number, x, are multiplied, the product is less than −4. What could x be?
 Ⓐ 0
 Ⓑ 2
 Ⓒ 1
 Ⓓ −2

20. The chart shows input and output. What rule changes each input to its output?

Input	Output
−3	−8
−1	−6
3	−2
1	−4

 Ⓕ add 5
 Ⓖ subtract 1
 Ⓗ add −5
 Ⓙ add −3

CHAPTER 2

Algebra

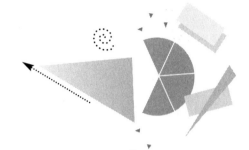

We commonly think of algebra as a separate course in middle or high school. However, algebraic reasoning is present in many concepts from the very early years of formal mathematics instruction. NCTM has helped identify these early forms of reasoning and now boldly refers to algebra as part of the recommended curriculum as early as pre-kindergarten. Regardless of the grade level, it is important to encourage students to investigate patterns, relationships, generalizations, properties, symbolism, and variables.

Algebraic concepts are usually formalized as students reach grades 6 and beyond. This book contains two sections for algebra: working with variables, and patterns. NCTM standards divide algebra expectations into four general categories when they state that instructional programs should enable students to:

✳ Understand patterns, relations, and functions

✳ Represent and analyze mathematical situations and structures using algebraic symbols

✳ Use mathematical models to represent and understand quantitative relationships

✳ Analyze change in various contexts

Following are the NCTM Standards for Algebra with accompanying expectations for grades 3–5 and 6–8.

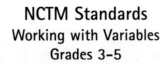

NCTM Standards
Working with Variables
Grades 3–5

Standards	Expectations
Understand patterns, relations, and functions	✳ Describe, extend, and make generalizations about geometric and numeric patterns; ✳ Represent and analyze patterns and functions, using words, tables, and graphs.
Represent and analyze mathematical situations and structures using algebraic symbols	✳ Identify such properties as commutativity, associativity, and distributivity, and use them to compute with whole numbers; ✳ Represent the idea of a variable as an unknown quantity using a letter or symbol; ✳ Express mathematical relationships using equations.
Use mathematical models to represent and understand quantitative relationships	✳ Model problem situations with objects and use representations such as graphs, tables, and equations to draw conclusions.
Analyze change in various contexts	✳ Investigate how a change in one variable relates to a change in a second variable; ✳ Identify and describe situations with constant or varying rates of change and compare them.

Standards	Expectations
Understand patterns, relations, and functions	✳ Represent, analyze, and generalize a variety of patterns with tables, graphs, words, and when possible, symbolic rules; ✳ Relate and compare different forms of representation for a relationship; ✳ Identify functions as linear or nonlinear and contrast their properties from tables, graphs, or equations.
Represent and analyze mathematical situations and structures using algebraic symbols	✳ Develop an initial conceptual understanding of different uses of variables; ✳ Explore relationships between symbolic expressions and graphs of lines, paying particular attention to the meaning of intercept and slope; ✳ Use symbolic algebra to represent situations and to solve problems, especially those that involve linear relationships; ✳ Recognize and generate equivalent forms for simple algebraic expressions and solve their linear equations.
Use mathematical models to represent and understand quantitative relationships	✳ Model and solve contextualized problems using various representations, such as graphs, tables, and equations.
Analyze change in various contexts	✳ Use graphs to analyze the nature of changes in quantities in linear relationships.

Working with Variables

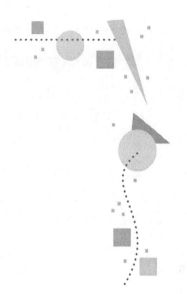

a variable is a symbol that represents a number. We sometimes refer to the variable in a problem as the unknown. Students often feel that problems with variables are "high-level" math, and most like the idea of "doing algebra." Finding the value of a variable can be a component of many different scenarios, from straight-forward if-then questions to complex story problems with identified givens and unknowns.

TEACHING TIPS

1. Discuss with students that finding the value of a variable is the same as solving any other kind of problem. The answer to any problem is the unknown.

2. Use a variety of symbols for variables, not just the traditional x and y.

3. Start teaching about variables by writing whole number, fraction, and decimal problems horizontally and putting a variable where the sum, difference, product, or quotient would be. For instance, write

$$\begin{array}{r} 146 \\ + \underline{29} \end{array} \text{ as } 146 + 29 = c.$$

Then ask the students to find c.
This eases students into the algebra habit.

Working with Variables

1. Don't let variables scare you! You have been solving problems for years that involve unknowns. *The answer in any problem can be thought of as the variable.*

2. To solve a word problem, *put the facts and the unknown in a math sentence.* Check the sentence to make sure it follows the logic of the word problem.

3. The steps you take toward solving for the value of a variable should lead you to *isolating the variable* (getting it by itself). We do this by "undoing" the operations in the math sentence. Sometimes we call this using the "opposite operation."

Working with Variables (4–5)

Test	pages 78–79														
	1	2	3	4	5	6	7	8	9	10	11	12	13	14	15
CAT	X	X	X	X	X										
MAT7	X	X	X	X	X	X	X	X	X	X	X	X	X		
SAT9	X	X	X	X	X	X				X					
Terra		X	X	X	X										
ESPA		X	X	X	X								X		
ISAT		X	X	X	X										
MCAS														X	X
NYS										X				X	
PACT	X	X	X	X	X							X		X	X
TASS	X	X	X	X	X									X	

Working with Variables (6–8)

Test	pages 80–81																	
	1	2	3	4	5	6	7	8	9	10	11	12	13	14	15	16	17	18
CAT	X			X														
IOWA			X				X	X				X						
MAT7	X	X				X												X
SAT9	X				X	X									X		X	X
Terra											X						X	
FCAT															X			X
GEPA	X												X			X	X	X
ISAT									X	X							X	
LEAP	X	X								X								X
MCAS		X			X								X		X			X
MEAP	X		X					X										X
NYS		X											X	X				
PACT												X			X	X		
TAAS	X														X			X

Grades 4–5

Working with Variables

If I subtract 4 from each side, then...

Choose the correct answer to each problem.

1. What number completes this table?

in	out
2	6
3	9
4	

Ⓐ 8   Ⓒ 12
Ⓑ 10   Ⓓ 14

2. Mark can rake 12 lawns on a Saturday. Which number sentence shows how many lawns Mark can rake in 4 Saturdays?
Ⓕ 12 ÷ 4 = ___
Ⓖ 12 x 4 = ___
Ⓗ ___ – 4 = 12
Ⓙ 12 – ___ = 4

3. In a pack of construction paper there are 26 sheets of blue paper and 14 sheets of purple. Which number sentence shows how many more blue sheets there are than purple sheets?
Ⓐ ___ x 14 = 26
Ⓑ 26 ÷ 14 = ___
Ⓒ 26 + 14 = ___
Ⓓ 26 – 14 = ___

4. There are 6 cooperative learning groups in Mr. Henderson's fifth grade class. Each group is made up of 4 students. Which number sentence shows how to find the total number of students in Mr. Henderson's class?
Ⓕ ___ ÷ 4 = 6
Ⓖ 6 x 4 = ___
Ⓗ 6 + 4 = ___
Ⓙ ___ – 4 = 6

5. There are 108 students going to the park for Field Day. Each van holds 9 students. Which number sentence shows how to find how many vans the school will need?
Ⓐ 108 – 9 = ___
Ⓑ 9 x 108 = ___
Ⓒ 108 ÷ 9 = ___
Ⓓ 108 + 9 = ___

6. If x = 3, then x + 3 =
Ⓕ 4   Ⓗ 9
Ⓖ 6   Ⓙ 12

7. If 155 + m = 260, then m =
- Ⓐ 75
- Ⓒ 105
- Ⓑ 95
- Ⓓ 415

8. If 75 + x = 200, then x =
- Ⓕ 175
- Ⓗ 125
- Ⓖ 150
- Ⓙ 110

9. If c = 8, then c – 3 =
- Ⓐ 24
- Ⓒ 5
- Ⓑ 11
- Ⓓ 4

10. If a – 12 = 248, then a =
- Ⓕ 124
- Ⓗ 250
- Ⓖ 236
- Ⓙ 260

11. If a = 48, then a ÷ 12 =
- Ⓐ 2
- Ⓒ 36
- Ⓑ 4
- Ⓓ 96

12. If 32 ÷ c = 4, then c =
- Ⓕ 6
- Ⓗ 9
- Ⓖ 8
- Ⓙ 16

13. If x – 340 = 694, then x =
- Ⓐ 54
- Ⓒ 836
- Ⓑ 354
- Ⓓ 1034

14. The rule for this input/output table is a + 4. Which two numbers complete the table?

a	7	13	19
a + 4	11		

- Ⓕ 12, 13
- Ⓗ 15, 19
- Ⓖ 17, 23
- Ⓙ 13, 15

15. What rule applies to this input/output table?

c	3	5	7
	6	10	14

- Ⓐ c x 2
- Ⓒ c + 5
- Ⓑ c + 3
- Ⓓ 7 + c

Grades 6–8

Working with Variables

To find y . . .

Choose the correct answer for each problem.

1. If 26 – x = 12 is an equation, what does x equal?
- Ⓐ 10
- Ⓑ 12
- Ⓒ 14
- Ⓓ 16

2. What does m have to be to make the equation 5(m + 6) = 45 correct?
- Ⓕ 9
- Ⓖ 3
- Ⓗ 1
- Ⓙ 0

3. What would c equal to make this a true number sentence?
6 + (5 x c) = 16
- Ⓐ 2
- Ⓑ 3
- Ⓒ 4
- Ⓓ 5

4. Which shows how to find the value of n in the equation n x 4 = 28?
- Ⓕ 28 x 4
- Ⓖ 28 ÷ 4
- Ⓗ 28 + 4
- Ⓙ 28 – 4

5. What value for c makes the equation 6c = 42 true?
- Ⓐ 2
- Ⓑ 4
- Ⓒ 7
- Ⓓ 14

6. If n = 9, what is the value of $\frac{3n + 11}{2}$?
- Ⓕ 7
- Ⓖ 14
- Ⓗ 19
- Ⓙ 25

7. What must c equal to make this a true number sentence?
4 x (3 + 5) = (4 x c) + (2 x 8)
- Ⓐ 2
- Ⓑ 3
- Ⓒ 4
- Ⓓ 6

8. Which equation shows n is 6 less than m divided by 4?
- Ⓕ n – 6 = m ÷ 4
- Ⓖ 6 – n = 4/m
- Ⓗ n – 6 = m/4
- Ⓙ n = m/4 – 6

9. Which number sentence expresses that 62 is 5 more than three times a number?
- Ⓐ 3n + 62 = 5
- Ⓑ 3n + 5 = 62
- Ⓒ 62 + 5 + 3n
- Ⓓ 3n + 62 = 5

10. Determine the value of m in the equation m – 6 = 14. In which equation is the value of c the same as the value of m?
- Ⓕ c + 3 = 17
- Ⓖ c – 17 = 3
- Ⓗ c ÷ 3 = 17
- Ⓙ c x 3 = 17

11. Which operation symbol would make this statement true?

If n + 14 = m, then n = m ___ 14.

(A) +   (C) x

(B) –   (D) ÷

12. Which symbol would replace ___ to make this equation true?

8 ___ 2 = 16

(F) +   (H) x

(G) –   (J) ÷

13. Both inequalities can be true if which number replaces c?

6 + c > 19   25 – c > 3

(A) 11   (C) 13

(B) 12   (D) 14

14. Adam drove 2 hours to Columbia, 112 miles from his home. What equation could he use to find his rate (r) of travel?

(F) r/2 = 112   (H) r = 112 + 2

(G) 112 – r = 2   (J) 2r = 112

15. Given this function table, what is Y when X is 8?

X	Y
1	4
2	7
3	10
4	13
5	16

(A) 11   (C) 24

(B) 13   (D) 25

16. The chart shows input and output. What rule changes each input to its output?

Input	Output
3	9
4	11
5	13
6	15

(F) multiply by 3

(G) add 6

(H) multiply by 4, then subtract 3

(J) multiply by 2, then add 3

17. Tesha bought 16 paperback books at the library sale for 25¢ each. Which number sentence expresses how much Tesha spent on books?

(A) 16 + .25 = ___   (C) 16 x .25 = ___

(B) 16 – .25 = ___   (D) 16 ÷ .25 = ___

18. Jennifer is making a table centerpiece that requires two pieces of ribbon, one 14 inches long and the other 22 inches long. After she cuts these two pieces she has some left over from the original piece that was 39 inches long. Which number sentence expresses how much ribbon was left over?

(F) 39 – ___ = 14

(G) 14 + 22 + 39 = ___

(H) 14 + 22 + ___ = 39

(J) 39 + ___ = 14 + 22

Patterns

*P*atterns are all around us. We need to point out patterns of all kinds to help students form the habit of recognizing them in a variety of contexts. Once students are comfortable with recognizing patterns, the next step is the extension and then creation of patterns.

TEACHING TIPS

1. Point out all kinds of patterns, both naturally occurring and created.

2. Give students many opportunities to both recognize and extend patterns.

3. Have students create their own patterns with objects, numbers, letters, symbols, etc.

4. Emphasize patterns all year long, not just when they occur in a textbook or curriculum plan.

Patterns

1. *Enjoy patterns!* Observe your surroundings and pick out patterns wherever you go.

2. Before attempting to extend a pattern, *carefully examine the pattern* several times to make sure you understand what makes the pattern work.

3. For word problems, *draw pictures* and *make charts* so you can see the pattern.

Patterns (4–5)

Test	pages 84–85											
	1	2	3	4	5	6	7	8	9	10	11	12
CAT					X							X
IOWA												
MAT7	X	X	X	X	X					X	X	X
SAT9					X	X						X
Terra									X			
FCAT					X							X
ESPA	X							X	X	X		
ISAT	X			X	X	X				X	X	X
LEAP								X				
MCAS												
MEAP								X				
NYS	X				X			X	X	X		X
PACT	X				X					X		X
TAAS	X		X	X		X	X			X	X	

Patterns (6–8)

Test	page 86						
	1	2	3	4	5	6	7
CAT	X						X
IOWA				X			
MAT7			X	X			X
SAT9							
Terra		X					
FCAT							
GEPA		X			X		X
ISAT							
LEAP	X						
MCAS		X					
MEAP	X						
NYS		X					
PACT	X		X				
TAAS	X					X	

Grades 4–5

Patterns

The next number in the pattern is …

Choose the correct answer for each problem.

1. What number is next in this number pattern?   4, 8, 12, 16, ____

Ⓐ 18   Ⓒ 24
Ⓑ 20   Ⓓ 26

2. Mrs. Michael's fourth grade class is having play practice before school for two weeks. If the pattern on the chart for the first week of school days continues into the next week, what is the first day of the second week when practice will begin at 8:15?

Play Practice	
Monday	8:30
Tuesday	8:15
Wednesday	No practice
Thursday	8:30
Friday	8:15

Ⓔ Monday   Ⓗ Wednesday
Ⓕ Tuesday   Ⓚ Thursday

3. What is the missing number in this pattern?
24, 21, 18, __, 12, 9

Ⓐ 16   Ⓒ 14
Ⓑ 15   Ⓓ 13

4. Samuel was making a pattern table for math class by gluing pennies to a piece of cardboard. He had 2 coins in the first row, 6 coins in the second row, 10 coins in the third row, and 14 coins in the fourth. If the pattern continues, which numbers belong in the blanks?
2, 6, 10, 14, ____, ____

Ⓔ 28, 30   Ⓗ 17, 20
Ⓕ 15, 19   Ⓚ 18, 22

5. How many squares will there be in the fifth figure in this pattern?

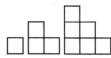

Ⓐ 9   Ⓒ 15
Ⓑ 12   Ⓓ 18

6. Which number fits in the ____ in this pattern?
58, 61, 64, ____, 70, 73

Ⓔ 67   Ⓗ 68
Ⓕ 65   Ⓚ 69

7. In the craft store, there are 8 sizes of packages of yarn. The largest is $1.80, the next largest is $1.60, the next largest is $1.40. At this rate, what will the smallest cost?

Ⓐ $.70   Ⓒ $.50
Ⓑ $.60   Ⓓ $.40

8. What is the rule for the following pattern?   4, 12, 36, ...

Ⓕ Add 8
Ⓖ Multiply by 2
Ⓗ Multiply by 3
Ⓙ Add 8, then 16

9. Which letter pattern matches the shape pattern?

✱ ❏ ✱ ✱ ❏ ❏ ✱ ✱ ✱ ❏ ❏ ❏

Ⓐ SBSSBBB
Ⓑ SBSSBBSSSBBB
Ⓒ SBSSBBSSBB
Ⓓ SBSSBBSBSB

10. What are the next two numbers in this pattern?

1, 2, 4, 8, 16, ___, ___

Ⓕ 32, 64   Ⓗ 18, 20
Ⓖ 20, 24   Ⓙ 32, 36

11. Juanita is very proud of her geode collection. Every time she visits her grandma in Colorado she adds to it. She has 5 shelves in her room for her collection. She decides to make a pattern of geodes on the shelves and complete the pattern the next time she goes to grandma's house. The first four shelves have 3, 7, 11, and 15 geodes. The fifth shelf is empty. How many geodes does she need to complete the pattern on the fifth shelf?

Ⓐ 16   Ⓒ 18
Ⓑ 17   Ⓓ 19

12. How many ✱ will there be in the sixth figure of this pattern?

Ⓕ 21   Ⓗ 30
Ⓖ 27   Ⓙ 36

Grades 6–8

Patterns

To complete the pattern...

Choose the correct answer for each problem.

1. What number completes the pattern 3, 7, 10, 14, 17, ____, 24?

   Ⓐ 20   Ⓒ 22
   Ⓑ 21   Ⓓ 23

2. What number comes next in this pattern?
   3, 9, 11, 17, 19, 25, ____
   Ⓕ 26   Ⓗ 28
   Ⓖ 27   Ⓙ 29

3. Which numbers would be next in the pattern?
   6, 12, 24, ____, ____, ____
   Ⓐ 30, 36, 42   Ⓒ 30, 42, 66
   Ⓑ 136, 48, 60   Ⓓ 48, 96, 192

4. Lanesha is in charge of creating a bulletin board. She wants to use colored stars as a border that follows a pattern alternating yellow, blue, and red. She uses 5 yellow, 9 blue, 13 red, 17 yellow, and so forth. If the pattern continues, what numbers of stars would she use?
   5, 9, 13, 17, ____, ____, ____
   Ⓕ 18, 19, 20   Ⓗ 19, 21, 23, 25
   Ⓖ 19, 21, 23   Ⓙ 21, 25, 29

5. Which number is the 21st in the sequence?
   5, 10, 15, 20...
   Ⓐ 100   Ⓒ 400
   Ⓑ 105   Ⓓ 500

6. For a conference, chairs were arranged in a large room. The front row had 7 chairs, the second had 10 chairs, and the third had 13 chairs. If this pattern continues, how many chairs will there be in the twelfth row?
   Ⓕ 37   Ⓗ 43
   Ⓖ 40   Ⓙ 46

7. A pattern is formed by groups of dots. How many dots would there be in the seventh group?

   ```
   *    * * *   * * * * *   * * * * * * *
   *     * *     * * *       * * * *
   *    * * *   * * * * *   * * * * * * *
   ```

   Ⓐ 21   Ⓒ 33
   Ⓑ 28   Ⓓ 39

CHAPTER 3

Geometry

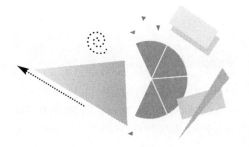

*g*eometry deals primarily with the properties and classification of shapes as well as how shapes relate to one another. Knowledge about points, lines, planes, angles, polygons, and spatial concepts fill the curriculum of geometry.

This book divides geometry into three topics:

✳ Perimeter and Area

✳ Angles and Their Measurement

✳ Assorted Topics in Geometry

The NCTM Standards divide geometry into four general categories, stating that instructional programs should enable all students to:

✳ Analyze characteristics and properties of two- and three-dimensional geometric shapes and develop mathematical arguments about geometric relationships

✳ Specify locations and describe spatial relationships using coordinate geometry and other representational systems

✳ Apply transformations and use symmetry to analyze mathematical situations

✳ Use visualization, spatial reasoning, and geometric modeling to solve problems

Following are the NCTM Standards for Geometry with accompanying expectations for grades 3–5 and 6–8.

NCTM Standards
Geometry
Grades 3–5

Standards	Expectations
Analyze characteristics and properties of two- and three-dimensional geometric shapes and develop mathematical arguments about geometric relationships	✳ Identify, compare, and analyze attributes of two- and three-dimensional shapes and develop vocabulary to describe the attributes; ✳ Classify two- and three-dimensional shapes according to their properties and develop definitions of classes of shapes such as triangles and pyramids; ✳ Investigate, describe, and reason about the results of subdividing, combining, and transforming shapes; ✳ Explore congruence and similarity; ✳ Make and test conjectures about geometric properties and relationships and develop logical arguments to justify conclusions.
Specify locations and describe spatial relationships using coordinate geometry and other representational systems	✳ Describe location and movement using common language and geometric vocabulary; ✳ Make and use coordinate systems to specify locations and to describe paths; ✳ Find the distance between points along horizontal and vertical lines of a coordinate system.
Apply transformations and use symmetry to analyze mathematical situations	✳ Predict and describe the results of sliding, flipping, and turning two-dimensional shapes; ✳ Describe a motion or series of motions that will show that two shapes are congruent; ✳ Identify and describe line and rotational symmetry in two- and three-dimensional shapes and designs.
Use visualization, spatial reasoning, and geometric modeling to solve problems	✳ Build and draw geometric objects; ✳ Create and describe mental images of objects, patterns, and paths; ✳ Identify and build a three-dimensional object from a two-dimensional object; ✳ Use geometric models to solve problems in other areas of mathematics, such as number and measurement; ✳ Recognize geometric ideas and relationships and apply them to other disciplines and to problems that arise in the classroom or in everyday life.

NCTM Standards
Geometry
Grades 6–8

Standards	Expectations
Analyze characteristics and properties of two- and three-dimensional geometric shapes and develop mathematical arguments about geometric relationships	✳ Precisely describe, classify, and understand relationships among types of two- and three-dimensional objects, using their defining properties; ✳ Understand relationships among the angles, side lengths, perimeters, areas, and volumes of similar objects; ✳ Create and critique inductive and deductive arguments concerning geometric ideas and relationships, such as congruence, similarity, and the Pythagorean relationship.
Specify locations and describe spatial relationships using coordinate geometry and other representational systems	✳ Use coordinate geometry to represent and examine the properties of geometric shapes; ✳ Use coordinate geometry to examine special geometric shapes, such as regular polygons or those with pairs of parallel or perpendicular sides.
Apply transformations and use symmetry to analyze mathematical situations	✳ Describe sizes, positions, and orientations of shapes under informal transformations such as flips, turns, slides, and scaling; ✳ Examine the congruence, similarity, and line or rotational symmetry of objects using transformations.
Use visualization, spatial reasoning, and geometric modeling to solve problems	✳ Draw geometric objects with specified properties, such as side lengths or angle measures; ✳ Use two-dimensional representations of three-dimensional objects to visualize and solve problems such as those involving surface area and volume; ✳ Use visual tools such as networks to represent and solve problems; ✳ Use geometric models to represent and explain numerical algebraic relationships; ✳ Recognize and apply geometric ideas and relationships in areas outside the mathematics classroom, such as art, science, and everyday life.

Perimeter and Area

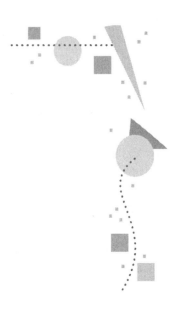

*P*erimeter and area are commonly thought of, and written about, in the context of geometry because of their spatial nature. They are fundamental concepts in the understanding of the characteristics and properties of two- and three-dimensional shapes and relationships. Drawing, classifying, and considering the definitions of shapes lead us naturally to the discovery of the importance and relevance of perimeter and area. Note that the most recent NCTM standards address perimeter and area in the measurement section. Please refer to the measurement standards in Chapter 4 (page 112) for student expectations.

TEACHING TIPS

1. Introduce and reinforce concepts with concrete objects, such as three-dimensional polyhedra and real-world examples. For example, illustrate a plane by referring to a desk top and a line segment by placing a pencil on the desk.

2. Habitually ask students to use geometric terms to describe familiar objects and relationships.

3. Make geometric concepts as visual as possible with classroom charts and manipulatives.

4. Rather than saving the discussion of geometry until it occurs in a book chapter or a special unit of study, "live geometry" on a daily basis with students to increase their awareness and comfort level.

1. *Look for geometry concepts all around you.* Give real-world objects and relationships geometric names. For instance, think of the wall meeting the floor as a right angle and a can of green beans as a cylinder.

2. Take time to *memorize geometric symbols and terms* such as < for angle, line segments as $\overline{AB}$, etc.

3. Learn how to *use formulas* for perimeter, area, and volume, so you can use them with confidence. Practicing in class will help you be ready to figure out how much carpet might be needed for your room or how much punch it would take to fill a bowl.

4. Learn to *recognize all the polygons.*

5. *Draw a picture* of what is described in geometry problems. For instance, if you are asked to find area, sketch a picture of the shape and label the parts you know.

Perimeter and Area (4–5)

Test	| pages 93–94													| page 95			
	1	2	3	4	5	6	7	8	9	10	11	12	13	1	2	3	4
CAT							X	X									
IOWA									X								
MAT7	X	X	X	X	X	X											
SAT9		X		X		X	X		X		X						
Terra													X				
ESPA														X			
FCAT																	
ISAT		X												X	X		
LEAP																	
MCAS																	
MEAP																	
NYS	X	X				X											X
PACT												X	X				
TAAS									X					X		X	

Perimeter and Area (6–8)

Test	pages 96–97													page 98			
	1	2	3	4	5	6	7	8	9	10	11	12	13	1	2	3	4
CAT											X	X					
IOWA															X		
MAT7													X	X			
SAT9																X	
Terra																	
FCAT										X							
GEPA							X			X							
ISAT				X													
LEAP	X			X													
MCAS			X		X												
MEAP	X		X														
NYS		X															X
PACT							X										
TAAS							X		X	X							

92

Grades 4–5

Perimeter and Area

The length times the width is ...

Choose the correct answer for each problem.

1. About how many small squares are needed to cover the entire rectangle?

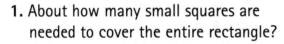

- Ⓐ 9
- Ⓑ 10
- Ⓒ 15
- Ⓓ 20

2. Jessica decided to build a fence around her garden. How much fencing will she need?

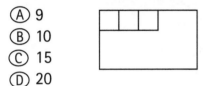

7 ft
2 ft
3 ft
2 ft
4 ft
4 ft

- Ⓕ 11 ft
- Ⓖ 17 ft
- Ⓗ 19 ft
- Ⓙ 22 ft

3. What is the area of the shaded part of the rectangle?

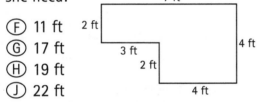

- Ⓐ 32 square units
- Ⓑ 12 square units
- Ⓒ 20 square units
- Ⓓ 22 square units

4. What is the perimeter of this figure?

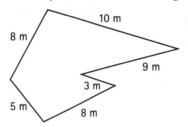

10 m
8 m
9 m
3 m
5 m
8 m

- Ⓕ 34m
- Ⓗ 64m
- Ⓖ 43m
- Ⓙ 72m

5. What is the area of a square that is 8 inches on each side?

- Ⓐ 8 in²
- Ⓒ 32 in²
- Ⓑ 16 in²
- Ⓓ 64 in²

6. What is the area of this rectangle?

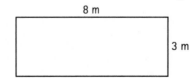

8 m
3 m

- Ⓕ 11 m²
- Ⓗ 24 m²
- Ⓖ 22 m²
- Ⓙ 48 m²

7. If the perimeter of a triangle is 48 inches and two of the sides measure 18 inches and 20 inches, what is the length of the third side?

(A) 10 inches

(B) 10 square inches

(C) 20 square inches

(D) 20 inches

8. What is the area of a tablecloth that is 84 inches long and 52 inches wide?

(F) 4,368 square inches

(G) 4,008 square inches

(H) 4,000 square inches

(J) 3,288 square inches

9. Julian wants to put an edging around a plain square tablecloth that is 5 feet on each side. How much edging will he need?

(A) 5 feet   (C) 20 feet

(B) 10 feet   (D) 25 feet

10. Ariel measured the front of a speaker box she wants for her room. If the rectangular box is 14 inches wide and 18 inches high, what is its perimeter?

(F) 32 inches   (H) 64 inches

(G) 72 inches   (J) 252 inches

11. What is the area of this figure?

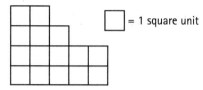

= 1 square unit

(A) 14 square units

(B) 15 square units

(C) 16 square units

(D) 20 square units

12. To find the area of a triangle, multiply $\frac{1}{2}$ times the product of the base and the height. What is the area of this triangle?

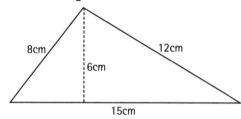

(F) 40 square cm

(G) 45 square cm

(H) 60 square cm

(J) 90 square cm

13. Claire wants to paint a 4 ft by 6 ft piece of wood. What is the area of the wood?

(A) 10 square ft

(B) 20 square ft

(C) 24 square ft

(D) 52 square ft

Grades 4–5

Perimeter and Area

To get the perimeter...

1. The length of a rectangular table is 8 ft. The perimeter of the table is 26 ft. What is the width?
   - (F) 5 feet
   - (G) 10 feet
   - (H) 16 feet
   - (J) 18 feet

2. A room is 12 feet long. The perimeter of the rectangular room is 40 feet. What is the area of the room?
   - (A) 62 square feet
   - (B) 96 square feet
   - (C) 336 square feet
   - (D) 480 square feet

3. What is the best estimate of the area of the shaded part of the grid?

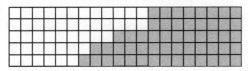

   - (F) 20 square units
   - (G) 32 square units
   - (H) 50 square units
   - (J) 64 square units

4. What is the area of this triangle?

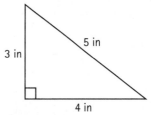

3 in   5 in   4 in

   - (A) 7 square inches
   - (B) 6 square inches
   - (C) 12 square inches
   - (D) 20 square inches

Grades 6–8

Perimeter and Area

To calculate the area...

Choose the correct answer for each problem.

1. This figure is a parallelogram. What is its perimeter?

   Ⓐ $7\frac{1}{4}$ cm

   Ⓑ 11 cm

   Ⓒ $6\frac{1}{4}$ cm

   Ⓓ $14\frac{1}{2}$ cm

   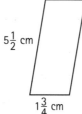

2. The perimeter of rectangle RSTU is 56 centimeters. What is the length of RS?

   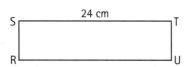

   Ⓕ 4 cm   Ⓗ 24 cm
   Ⓖ 5.6 cm   Ⓙ 48 cm

3. Using the formula A = *lw*, how does area change if length is tripled and width is doubled?
   Ⓐ The area doubles
   Ⓑ The area triples
   Ⓒ The area is four times as great
   Ⓓ The area is six times as great

4. What is the perimeter of a regular hexagon with one side 12 centimeters long?
   Ⓕ 6 cm   Ⓗ 72 cm
   Ⓖ 12 cm   Ⓙ 144 cm

5. What is the area of the porch Shania is planning to build with her dad?

   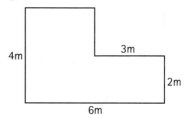

   Ⓐ 18 m²   Ⓒ 12 m²
   Ⓑ 15 m²   Ⓓ 10 m²

6. A frame measures 9 inches wide and 11 inches long. The opening for the picture is 5 inches by 7 inches. Which expression represents the area of the wooden frame?

   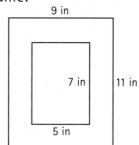

   Ⓕ (9 – 5) x (11 – 7)
   Ⓖ (11 – 9) x (7 – 5)
   Ⓗ (11 – 9)² x (7 – 5)²
   Ⓙ (9 x 11) – (5 x 7)

7. Which polygon does not have an area of 36 square centimeters?

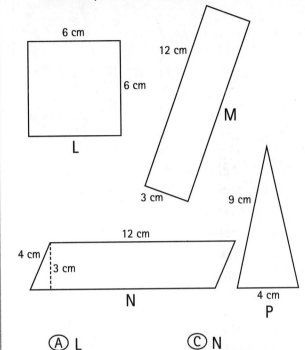

6 cm

6 cm

12 cm

M

L

3 cm

9 cm

12 cm

4 cm

3 cm

N

4 cm

P

Ⓐ L   Ⓒ N
Ⓑ M   Ⓓ P

8. Marilyn's desk is 2.5 feet by 1.75 feet. What is the surface area of her desk?
Ⓕ .75 ft²   Ⓗ 4.375 ft²
Ⓖ 4.25 ft²   Ⓙ 8.5 ft²

9. What is the area of this rectangle?

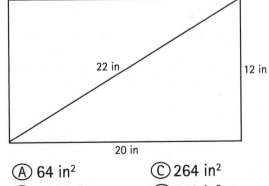

22 in   12 in

20 in

Ⓐ 64 in²   Ⓒ 264 in²
Ⓑ 240 in²   Ⓓ 440 in²

10. Jeff and Sandy volunteered to decorate the hall bulletin board. They first covered the entire 4 feet by 9 feet surface with white paper. Now they want to cover the white paper completely, without gaps or overlaps, with colored sticky notes that are 3 inches by 3 inches. They will write a message under each sticky note. How many messages will they write?
Ⓕ 48   Ⓗ 324
Ⓖ 144   Ⓙ 576

11. The perimeter of a rectangle is 40 centimeters. Which of the following could be the length and width of the rectangle?
Ⓐ 4 cm by 20 cm
Ⓑ 12 cm by 16 cm
Ⓒ 10 cm by 8 cm
Ⓓ 8 cm by 12 cm

12. What is the perimeter of a game table that is 6 feet by 4 feet?
Ⓕ 64   Ⓗ 20
Ⓖ 24   Ⓙ 10

13. What is the area of this rectangle?
Ⓐ 70 cubic inches
Ⓑ 17 cubic inches
Ⓒ 34 square inches
Ⓓ 70 square inches

7 in

10 in

Grades 6–8

Perimeter and Area

For a triangle,
$A = \frac{1}{2} bh \dots$

1. What is the area of a piece of poster-board that is 27 centimeters long and 18 centimeters wide?
   - Ⓕ 45 square centimeters
   - Ⓖ 90 square centimeters
   - Ⓗ 600 square centimeters
   - Ⓙ 486 square centimeters

2. In the rectangle, the area of the shaded portion is 10 square centimeters. If the height is 5 centimeters, what is the length of the base?

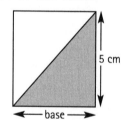

5 cm

←— base —→

   - Ⓐ 4
   - Ⓑ 5
   - Ⓒ 10
   - Ⓓ 15

3. What is the area of triangle KMN? Use $A = \frac{1}{2} bh$

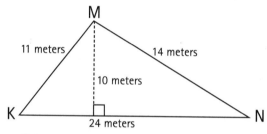

M

11 meters   14 meters

10 meters

K   24 meters   N

   - Ⓕ 59 square meters
   - Ⓖ 120 square meters
   - Ⓗ 140 square meters
   - Ⓙ 240 square meters

4. If eight 1 cm squares are put together, what is the smallest perimeter possible?

1 cm

1 cm

   - Ⓐ 12 cm
   - Ⓒ 16 cm
   - Ⓑ 14 cm
   - Ⓓ 18 cm

Angles and Their Measurement

*t*he study of angles includes drawing, constructing, comparing, classifying, and measuring them. In grades 4–5 students concentrate on recognizing angles as acute, obtuse, and right. They also develop a sense of estimation of angle measurements as they learn how to use a protractor. In grades 6–8 angles are put into the specific context of triangles and other polygons, with emphasis on angle relationships. As with perimeter and area, the study of angles is typically considered a topic in geometry, but the student expectations for the measurement of angles is in the measurement standards in Chapter 4 (page 112).

Angles and Their Measurement (4–5)

Test	pages 100			
	1	2	3	4
CAT	X	X		
IOWA				
MAT7				
SAT9	X	X		
Terra				
FCAT				
GEPA				
ISAT			X	X
LEAP				
MCAS				
MEAP				
NYS				
PACT				
TAAS				

Angles and Their Measurement (6–8)

Test	page 101–102											
	1	2	3	4	5	6	7	8	9	10	11	12
CAT		X										
IOWA												
MAT7	X											
SAT9	X											
Terra												
FCAT				X	X	X			X			X
GEPA	X							X				
ISAT												
LEAP									X		X	
MCAS	X								X	X		
MEAP									X		X	
NYS	X			X								
PACT												
TAAS			X									

Grades 4–5

Angles and Their Measurement

A right angle has 90°, so...

Choose the correct answer to each problem.

1. Which angle appears to be a right angle?

   Ⓐ M   Ⓑ N   Ⓒ O   Ⓓ P

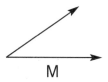   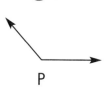

       M   N   O   P

2. How many right angles does this polygon appear to have?

   Ⓕ 1   Ⓖ 2   Ⓗ 3   Ⓙ 4

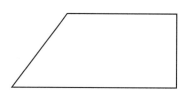

3. One angle of a right triangle is 35°. What is the measure of the other acute angle?

   Ⓐ 35°   Ⓑ 45°   Ⓒ 55°   Ⓓ 90°

4. What is the best estimate of the measure of <LMN?

   Ⓕ 10°   Ⓖ 20°   Ⓗ 40°   Ⓙ 60°

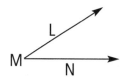

Grades 6–8

Angles and Their Measurement

To find the compliment of <XYZ...

Choose the correct answer to each problem.

1. Which angle appears to be an obtuse angle?

Ⓐ   Ⓑ   Ⓒ   Ⓓ

2. What kind of angle does <BAC appear to be?

Ⓕ right   Ⓗ straight
Ⓖ obtuse   Ⓙ acute

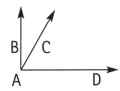

3. Which of these must contain a 90° angle?

Ⓐ an equilateral triangle   Ⓒ a right triangle
Ⓑ a scalene triangle   Ⓓ an isosceles triangle

4. Triangle XYZ is a right triangle. Which two angles are complementary?

Ⓕ <XYZ and <YXZ   Ⓗ <YXZ and <XZY
Ⓖ <XZY and <YXZ   Ⓙ <XZY and <XYZ

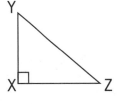

5. What is the measure of angle M?

Ⓐ 50°   Ⓒ 60°
Ⓑ 55°   Ⓓ 65°

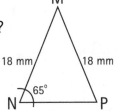

18 mm   18 mm
65°
N   P

6. Which polygon must contain two acute angles?

Ⓕ parallelogram   Ⓖ right triangle   Ⓗ pentagon   Ⓙ rectangle

7. If angles A and B are supplementary and angle A has measure 48°, what is the measure of angle B?

Ⓐ 42°　　　　Ⓑ 48°　　　　Ⓒ 132°　　　　Ⓓ 142°

8. What is the measure of <B in this right isosceles triangle?

Ⓕ 40°　　　　Ⓗ 60°
Ⓖ 45°　　　　Ⓙ 90°

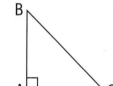

9. What is the measure of <M if the measure of <P is 110° and the measure of <N is 40°?

Ⓐ 30°　　　　Ⓒ 40°
Ⓑ 38°　　　　Ⓓ 42°

10. Lines M and N are parallel. What is the measure of X?

Ⓕ 150°　　　　Ⓗ 50°
Ⓖ 130°　　　　Ⓙ 40°

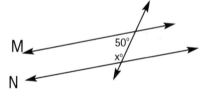

11. What is the best estimate of the number of degrees in angle NMP?

Ⓐ 40°　　　　Ⓒ 60°
Ⓑ 100°　　　　Ⓓ 120°

12. What is the measure of angle M?

Ⓕ 70°　　　　Ⓗ 80°
Ⓖ 75°　　　　Ⓙ 85°

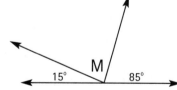

Assorted Topics in Geometry

*g*eometry is a rich part of mathematics. In addition to the main topics of perimeter, area, and angles, there are many other important concepts that have been grouped in this section. These include:

* parallel and perpendicular lines
* line segments
* polygons, circles, and geometric solids
* similarity and congruency
* symmetry
* volume
* coordinate planes

Including these topics in a study of geometry is essential to success on standardized tests.

Assorted Topics in Geometry (4–5)

Test	pages 105–106													page 107					
	1	2	3	4	5	6	7	8	9	10	11	12	13	1	2	3	4	5	6
CAT	X				X			X											
IOWA	X				X				X										
MAT7	X	X	X	X	X	X	X											X	X
SAT9									X	X						X			
Terra	X	X			X		X					X				X	X		
FCAT			X			X			X		X								
ESPA	X		X			X	X				X	X							
ISAT														X	X	X			
LEAP		X												X					
MCAS												X							
MEAP		X												X					
NYS						X				X	X	X							X
PACT									X	X		X							
TAAS		X		X								X							

Assorted Topics in Geometry (6–8)

Test	pages 108–109														
	1	2	3	4	5	6	7	8	9	10	11	12	13	14	15
CAT					X										
IOWA					X										
MAT7															
SAT9															
Terra															
FCAT	X													X	
GEPA						X									
ISAT															X
LEAP								X							X
MCAS			X							X					
MEAP								X							X
NYS		X					X								
PACT												X			
TAAS				X					X	X					

Assorted Topics in Geometry (6–8)

Test	pages 110–111											
	1	2	3	4	5	6	7	8	9	10	11	12
CAT					X							
IOWA					X							
MAT7												
SAT9	X											
Terra												
FCAT												
GEPA						X						
ISAT												
LEAP												
MCAS												
MEAP												
NYS												
PACT								X				
TAAS			X							X		

Grades 4–5

Assorted Topics in Geometry

Choose the correct answer to each problem.

1. Which lines appear to be parallel?
Ⓐ RS and TV   Ⓑ RS and SV   Ⓒ RT and SV   Ⓓ RT and RS

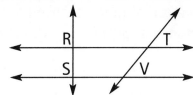

2. Which pair of shapes appear to be congruent?
Ⓕ M   Ⓖ N   Ⓗ P   Ⓙ Q

 M    N   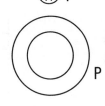 P   Q

3. What is the name of this figure?
Ⓐ pentagon   Ⓒ quadrilateral
Ⓑ parallelogram   Ⓓ octagon

4. Which does *not* show a line of symmetry?
Ⓕ L   Ⓖ M   Ⓗ N   Ⓙ P

L
M
N
P

5. Which figure(s) show lines that intersect?
Ⓐ M and P   Ⓒ L and N
Ⓑ N   Ⓓ All of them

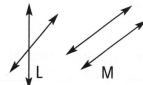
L   M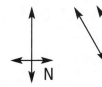
N   P

Name _____

6. Which polygon is a trapezoid?

   Ⓕ L   Ⓖ M   Ⓗ N   Ⓙ P

7. Which line segments intersect?

   Ⓐ LM and PK   Ⓒ ST and LM
   Ⓑ NR and ST   Ⓓ NR and PK

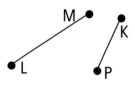 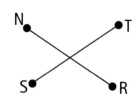

8. Which of these is most like a can of green beans?

   Ⓕ cylinder   Ⓖ rectangular prism   Ⓗ cube   Ⓙ sphere

9. Which is *not* a parallelogram?

   Ⓐ M   Ⓒ P
   Ⓑ N   Ⓓ R

10. What is the ordered pair that names M?

   Ⓕ (4, 1)   Ⓗ (1, 4)
   Ⓖ (3, 2)   Ⓙ (6, 3)

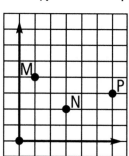

11. What is the volume of this rectangular prism?

   Ⓐ 32 cubic cm   Ⓒ 60 cubic cm
   Ⓑ 96 cubic cm   Ⓓ 15 cubic cm

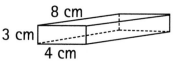

12. Which pair of numbers represents the number of edges and number of faces of this figure?

   Ⓕ 4, 8   Ⓗ 16, 8
   Ⓖ 8, 4   Ⓙ 12, 6

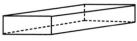

13. Which shape is congruent to the shaded part of this figure?

   Ⓐ M   Ⓒ N
   Ⓑ L   Ⓓ Both L and N

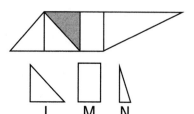

Name _____

Grades 4–5

Assorted Topics in Geometry

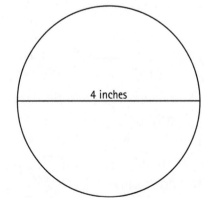

1. What is the new ordered pair if point A is now (4, 3) and it is moved 1 unit to the right and 2 units up?
   - (F) (4, 4)
   - (H) (4, 2)
   - (G) (5, 5)
   - (J) (1, 3)

2. If triangle LMN is similar to triangle PQR, what is the length of PR?
   - (A) 9m
   - (C) 7m
   - (B) 8m
   - (D) 6m

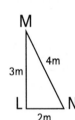 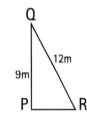

3. How many sides does a hexagon have?
   - (F) 6
   - (G) 7
   - (H) 8
   - (J) 9

4. Which two line segments appear to be perpendicular?
   - (A) P and Q
   - (C) N and P
   - (B) M and Q
   - (D) L and M

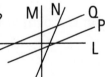

5. Ariel was measuring the size of the tires on her bicycle. The radius of the wheel was 13 inches. What is the diameter of the wheel?
   - (F) 14 inches
   - (G) 7 inches
   - (H) 26 inches
   - (J) 39 inches

6. What is the radius of this circle?
   - (A) 2 inches
   - (C) 6 inches
   - (B) 4 inches
   - (D) 8 inches

4 inches

Grades 6–8

Assorted Topics in Geometry

If two shapes are congruent, then...

Choose the correct answer for each problem.

1. Which polygon always has four congruent sides?
  (A) rectangle   (B) trapezoid   (C) parallelogram   (D) rhombus

2. Which of these figures has exactly six sides?
  (F) quadrilateral   (G) pentagon   (H) octagon   (J) hexagon

3. What can you conclude about isosceles triangle MNP if MN = MP?
  (A) NM ≠ PM   (C) Angles M and N are congruent
  (B) Angle M is 90°   (D) Angles N and P are congruent

4. What characteristic separates pentagons and hexagons?
  (F) measure of angles   (H) area
  (G) number of sides   (J) number of faces

5. Which polygon is a pentagon?
  (A) L   (B) M   (C) N   (D) P

  L   M   N   P

6. Which triangle is obtuse?
  (F) R   (G) S   (H) T   (J) V

  R   S   T   V

7. Which quadrilaterals are similar?
  (A) L and M only
  (B) L and N only
  (C) L, M, and N
  (D) M and N only

  2cm [L]   6cm [M]   6cm [N]
      6cm   6cm   18cm

Name _____

8. If triangle MNP is congruent to triangle SRT, then _____.

     Ⓕ MN = ST   Ⓗ NP = RS

     Ⓖ <MNP = <SRT   Ⓙ <MPN = <SRT

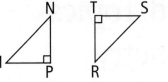

9. Triangles HJK and LMN are similar.

What line segment completes the proportion $\frac{HJ}{LM} = \frac{JK}{}$?

     Ⓐ JK   Ⓒ MN

     Ⓑ LN   Ⓓ LM

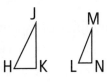

10. Triangles XYZ and FGH are similar. What is the length of FG?

     Ⓕ 18   Ⓗ 12

     Ⓖ 16   Ⓙ 9

11. Emily bought a jewelry box that is 3 inches high, 7 inches long, and 4 inches wide. How many cubic inches of space does the box have?

     Ⓐ 84 in³   Ⓑ 40 in³   Ⓒ 33 in³   Ⓓ 14 in³

12. What is the volume of this rectangular prism?

     Ⓕ 19 m3   Ⓗ 78 m3

     Ⓖ 38 m3   Ⓙ 240 m3

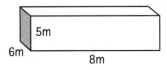

13. What is the volume of a rectangular prism that is 4 cm high, 8 cm long, and 5 cm wide?

     Ⓐ 17 cubic cm   Ⓒ 40 cubic cm

     Ⓑ 32 cubic cm   Ⓓ 160 cubic cm

14. Which figure contains a vertical line of symmetry?

     Ⓕ L   Ⓖ M   Ⓗ N   Ⓙ P

15. Which figure has exactly four lines of symmetry?

     Ⓐ L   Ⓑ M   Ⓒ N   Ⓓ P

Percentage Correct = $\dfrac{\text{\# correct}}{\text{total \#}}$ = ____%

Grades 6–8

Assorted Topics in Geometry

The coordinates of part A are...

1. How many lines of symmetry does this figure have?

   Ⓕ 1   Ⓗ 3
   Ⓖ 2   Ⓙ 4

2. Which figure has only one line of symmetry?

   Ⓐ L   Ⓑ M   Ⓒ N   Ⓓ P

    L   M   N   P

3. Figure CDRS is a parallelogram. Three vertices have coordinates C (2, 4), D (4, 7), and R (9, 7). What ordered pair represents S?

   Ⓕ (7, 4)   Ⓗ (7, 9)
   Ⓖ (4, 9)   Ⓙ (4, 7)

   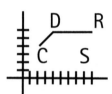

4. What ordered pair names A?

   Ⓐ (4, −4)   Ⓒ (−4, 4)
   Ⓑ (−4, −4)   Ⓓ (4, 4)

   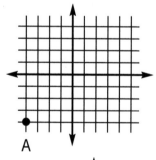

5. Which letter in the coordinate plane names the ordered pair (2, −5)?

   Ⓕ L   Ⓗ S
   Ⓖ M   Ⓙ T

   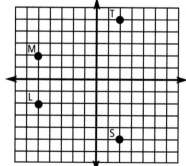

6. Which lines are parallel?

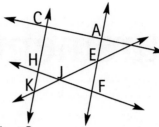

    Ⓐ KE and HJ   Ⓒ CK and HJ

    Ⓑ KE and AF   Ⓓ CK and AF

7. Which example illustrates perpendicular lines?

    Ⓕ L   Ⓖ M   Ⓗ N   Ⓙ P

    L   M   N   P

8. In the circle, if BC is 26 inches and N is the centerpoint, how long is NM?

    Ⓐ 26 inches   Ⓒ 52 inches

    Ⓑ 13 inches   Ⓓ 15 inches

9. What is the radius of this circle?

    Ⓕ 4 feet   Ⓗ 32 feet

    Ⓖ 8 feet   Ⓙ about 48 feet

16 feet

10. A 33-$\frac{1}{3}$ rpm record has a radius of 6 inches. What is its diameter?

    Ⓐ 7 inches   Ⓑ 12 inches   Ⓒ 36 inches   Ⓓ 39$\frac{1}{3}$ inches

11. If the radius of a circle is doubled, how is the circumference changed?

    Ⓕ $\frac{1}{2}$ as large   Ⓖ 2 times as large   Ⓗ 3 times as large   Ⓙ no change

12. Choose the line segment that is the diameter of the circle.

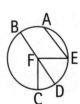

    Ⓐ CF   Ⓑ BD   Ⓒ AE   Ⓓ EF

CHAPTER 4

Measurement

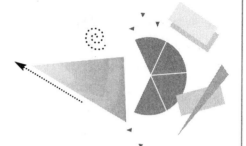

When we check the temperature in the morning, prepare ingredients for our evening meal, and perform any number of daily tasks in between, we are using the tools of measurement. The process of measurement is how we quantify and make sense of our world, and it is never too early to present measurement concepts to students.

Measurement and geometry are closely linked; concepts about how shapes are formed and relate to one another become concrete when we apply measurement techniques. Measurement serves as the means by which students explore and understand concepts of geometry, and, in a broader sense, the physical world around them.

The NCTM standards divide measurement into two general categories when they state that instructional programs should enable students to:

✳ Understand measurable attributes of objects and the units, systems, and processes of measurement

✳ Apply appropriate techniques, tools, and formulas to determine measurements

Following are the NCTM Standards for Measurement with accompanying expectations for grades 3–5 and 6–8.

NCTM Standards
Measurement
Grades 3–5

Standards	Expectations
Understand measurable attributes of objects and the units, systems, and processes of measurements	✳ Understand such attributes as length, area, weight, volume, and size of angle, and select the appropriate type of unit for measuring each attribute; ✳ Understand the need for measuring with standard units and become familiar with standard units in the customary and metric systems; ✳ Carry out simple unit conversions, such as from centimeters to meters, within a system of measurement; ✳ Understand that measurements are approximations and understand how differences in units affect precision; ✳ Explore what happens to measurements of a two-dimensional shape, such as its perimeter and area, when the shape is changed in some way.
Apply appropriate techniques, tools, and formulas to determine measurements	✳ Develop strategies for estimating the perimeters, areas, and volumes of irregular shapes; ✳ Select and apply appropriate standard units and tools to measure length, area, volume, weight, time, temperature, and the size of angles; ✳ Select and use benchmarks to estimate measurements; ✳ Develop, understand, and use formulas to find the area of rectangles and related triangles and parallelograms; ✳ Develop strategies to determine the surface areas and volumes of rectangular solids.

Standards	Expectations
Understand measurable attributes of objects and the units, systems, and processes of measurement	✳ Understand both metric and customary systems of measurement; ✳ Understand relationships among units and convert from one unit to another within the same system; ✳ Understand, select, and use units of appropriate size and type to measure angles, perimeter, area, surface area, and volume.
Apply appropriate techniques, tools, and formulas to determine measurements	✳ Use common benchmarks to select appropriate methods for estimating measurements; ✳ Select and apply techniques and tools to accurately find length, area, volume, and angle measures at appropriate levels of precision; ✳ Develop and use formulas to determine circumferences of circles and areas of triangles, parallelograms, trapezoids, and circles, and develop strategies to find the area of more complex shapes; ✳ Develop strategies to determine the surface area and volume of selected prisms, pyramids, and cylinders; ✳ Solve problems involving scale factors, using ratio and proportion; ✳ Solve simple problems involving rates and derived measurements for such attributes as velocity and density.

1. Emphasize the practicality of measurement.

2. Point out aspects of measurement wherever and whenever they occur.

3. Display many posters of measures and their applications.

4. Give equal amounts of practice using both the U.S. customary system and the metric system.

5. Relate U.S. customary measures to the metric system in broad ways to allow students to estimate from one to the other.

6. Emphasize units and conversion among units within both the U.S. customary system and the metric system.

7. Talk often about reasonableness of answers. Equip students with easy to remember examples that make measurement amounts realistic. For instance, the diameter of the eye's iris is about a centimeter, and a yard is about the distance from your nose to the end of your fingers when your arm is stretched straight out to the side.

SUPER SUCCESS STRATEGIES

1. Know the *basic units* of measurements and *what they measure* in both the U.S. customary system and the metric system.

2. *Practice converting from unit to unit in the U.S. customary system.* For instance, know that 4 quarts equal 1 gallon, so 12 quarts equal 3 gallons.

3. *Practice converting in the metric system* by understanding that length, volume, mass, and weight use powers of 10. For instance, 1 meter equals 100 centimeters.

4. *Estimate* measurements and then actually measure to see how close you can come.

5. *Practice reading clocks* and mentally adding and subtracting minutes and hours.

6. Think about all the ways *measurement affects our lives.* Watch for examples!

Measurement (4–5)

Test	pages 117–118																
	1	2	3	4	5	6	7	8	9	10	11	12	13	14	15	16	17
CAT						X					X	X					
IOWA	X	X	X			X							X				
MAT7	X	X	X	X	X	X	X	X	X	X	X						
SAT9			X	X		X	X	X			X			X			
Terra					X						X						
FCAT				X			X	X				X			X		
ESPA	X	X		X		X	X										
ISAT																	X
LEAP				X													
MCAS						X									X	X	
MEAP				X													
NYS						X								X			
PACT																	
TAAS										X	X					X	

Measurement (6–8)

Test	pages 119–120															
	1	2	3	4	5	6	7	8	9	10	11	12	13	14	15	16
CAT													X			
IOWA			X													
MAT7		X							X							
SAT9			X				X					X	X			
Terra					X	X										
FCAT				X						X						X
GEPA					X				X					X		
ISAT								X					X			
LEAP	X				X				X				X			
MCAS			X	X	X					X	X					X
MEAP	X				X			X					X			
NYS		X										X				X
PACT																
TAAS				X												

Grades 4–5

Measurement

If there are 3 feet in a yard...

Choose the correct answer for each problem.

1. Which unit would you use to measure the amount of punch in a bowl?
- (A) gram
- (B) meter
- (C) liter
- (D) kiloliter

2. Which unit would you use to measure the length of a skateboard?
- (F) inch
- (G) yard
- (H) meter
- (J) gram

3. Mickey was eating lunch four and one-half hours after his morning alarm rang at 7:30 AM. Which digital clock shows Mickey's lunch time?

L (11:45)   M (12:00)

N (12:15)   P (12:30)

- (A) L
- (B) M
- (C) N
- (D) P

4. Which unit is best used to describe the weight of a railroad car?
- (F) ounce
- (G) ton
- (H) gram
- (J) meter

5. How many quarts are made up of 12 cups?
- (A) 12
- (B) 8
- (C) 4
- (D) 3

6. What time will it be in 40 minutes?

- (F) 8:05
- (G) 8:00
- (H) 7:55
- (J) 7:45

7. The length of a paper clip is closest to ___?
- (A) 1 foot
- (B) 1 inch
- (C) 1 meter
- (D) 1 centimeter

8. On a standard-size dining table the distance from the floor to the top is closest to ___:
- (F) 6 feet
- (G) 4 feet
- (H) 3 feet
- (J) 2 feet

9. 1 kilogram=
- (A) 1000 centimeters
- (B) 1 liter
- (C) 100 grams
- (D) 1000 grams

10. 1 liter=
- Ⓕ 1000 grams
- Ⓖ 1000 milliliters
- Ⓗ 1000 kiloliters
- Ⓙ 1000 ounces

11. Which measurement is the greatest amount?
- Ⓐ 1 gallon
- Ⓑ 6 cups
- Ⓒ 5 quarts
- Ⓓ 7 pints

12. Which unit is used to measure mass?
- Ⓕ liters
- Ⓖ meters
- Ⓗ grams
- Ⓙ quarts

13. Marita is making soup. Her recipe calls for a quart of water. What measurement is closest to a quart?
- Ⓐ kilogram
- Ⓑ gallon
- Ⓒ pint
- Ⓓ liter

14. Janie begins her piano lesson at 3:45. It lasts until 5:00. How long is her lesson?
- Ⓕ 45 minutes
- Ⓖ 55 minutes
- Ⓗ 75 minutes
- Ⓙ 90 minutes

15. The bag of oranges weighed between 2 and 3 pounds. Which of these could be the weight of the oranges in ounces? (1 pound = 16 ounces)
- Ⓐ 20 ounces
- Ⓑ 30 ounces
- Ⓒ 40 ounces
- Ⓓ 50 ounces

16. J.P. swam across the pond as fast as he could. He swam for 120 seconds. How many minutes is this?
- Ⓕ 2
- Ⓖ 3
- Ⓗ 4
- Ⓙ 6

17. For a class pizza party, Ms. Lawson bought five 2-liter bottles of soda. How many milliliters is this?
- Ⓐ 10,000 ml
- Ⓑ 5000 ml
- Ⓒ 2000 ml
- Ⓓ 1000 ml

Grades 6–8

Measurement

To measure the width of the book...

Choose the correct answer for each problem.

1. What is the best estimate of the height of your desk?
- Ⓐ 9 decimeters
- Ⓒ 9 meters
- Ⓑ 9 centimeters
- Ⓓ 9 grams

2. The length of the longest side of a videotape is about _____.
- Ⓕ 2 inches
- Ⓗ 1 yard
- Ⓖ 1 foot
- Ⓙ 8 inches

3. The area of a videotape is best measured in _____.
- Ⓐ square yards
- Ⓒ square inches
- Ⓑ square feet
- Ⓓ square meters

4. Ryan lives 6 kilometers from school. How many meters is this?
- Ⓕ .6 m
- Ⓗ 600 m
- Ⓖ 60 m
- Ⓙ 6000 m

5. How many centimeters are there in 250 meters?
- Ⓐ 25 cm
- Ⓒ 25,000 cm
- Ⓑ 2,500 cm
- Ⓓ 250,000 cm

6. There are 100 centimeters in a meter and 1000 meters in a kilometer. How many centimeters are there in one kilometer?
- Ⓕ 1,000 cm
- Ⓗ 100,000 cm
- Ⓖ 10,000 cm
- Ⓙ 1,000,000 cm

7. The teacher's desk is 72 inches from the door. How many feet is that?
- Ⓐ 7.2 feet
- Ⓒ 6.5 feet
- Ⓑ 7.0 feet
- Ⓓ 6.0 feet

8. Which is the greatest distance?
- Ⓕ 300 meters
- Ⓖ 3000 centimeters
- Ⓗ 500 decimeters
- Ⓙ .5 kilometer

9. About how many feet tall is a bedroom door?
- Ⓐ 5 feet
- Ⓒ 12 feet
- Ⓑ 7 feet
- Ⓓ 15 feet

10. How many cups are in one quart?
- (F) 6
- (G) 4
- (H) 3
- (J) 2

11. Hector is making sopapillas for his class. A dozen requires $\frac{1}{2}$ cup of milk. He has a pint of milk. How many can he make before he will need more milk?
- (A) 48
- (B) 42
- (C) 36
- (D) 24

12. A large mug holds 2 cups of soda. If a pitcher holds 3 quarts, how many mugs could be filled from a full pitcher?
- (F) 6
- (G) 9
- (H) 12
- (J) 16

13. Track practice will be over 1 hour and 35 minutes after the last bell rings at 3:10 p.m. What time will practice end?
- (A) 3:45
- (B) 4:10
- (C) 4:45
- (D) 4:55

14. On Thanksgiving Day, Grace's family watched the Macy's Parade from 9:00 a.m. to 10:30 a.m., a football game from 1:00 p.m. to 3:30 p.m., and a special holiday variety show from 7:30 p.m. to 9:30 p.m. How many minutes did they watch television?
- (F) 90 minutes
- (G) 180 minutes
- (H) 300 minutes
- (J) 360 minutes

15. At noon it was 17°F. The temperature began to drop quickly at dark. By 9 p.m., it was −12°F. How many degrees had the temperature dropped from noon to 9 p.m.?
- (A) −5°
- (B) 5°
- (C) 17°
- (D) 29°

16. Jonathan's art assignment is to make a scale drawing of a billboard located on the highway just outside his town. He called the company that owns the large sign and found out that it is 30 feet by 20 feet. Jonathan's poster board is 17 inches by 11 inches. He decides to use a scale of 1 inch = 2 feet. What will the dimensions of his scale drawing be?
- (F) 13 inches by 9 inches
- (G) 3 feet by 2 feet
- (H) 15 inches by 10 inches
- (J) 1 inch by 2 feet

CHAPTER 5

Data Analysis and Probability

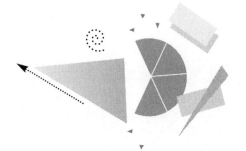

*t*elevision, radio, newspapers, magazines, the Internet—these media bombard us with facts and figures every day. Students need data analysis tools to organize, analyze, and evaluate all this information, and they must be able to effectively and efficiently represent data in ways that will make sense to an audience. The NCTM standards state that students should be able to:

✳ Formulate questions that can be addressed with data, and collect, organize, and display relevant data to answer them

✳ Select and use appropriate statistical methods to analyze data

✳ Develop and evaluate inferences and predictions that are based on data

Probability concepts are important in modern life because we constantly make decisions about how to use the massive amount of information we face each day. The NCTM standards state that students should be able to:

✳ Understand and apply basic concepts of probability

This book contains problems in both data analysis and probability. The data analysis section includes concepts of graph and chart reading, mean, median, mode, and range. The probability and combination section includes probability as determined by random selection using cards, number cubes, spinners, and real-object selection. It also includes the concept of creating combinations among various items or people.

Following are the NCTM Standards for Data Analysis and Probability with accompanying expectations for grades 3–5 and 6–8.

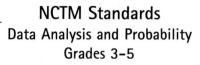

NCTM Standards
Data Analysis and Probability
Grades 3-5

Standards	Expectations
Formulate questions that can be addressed with data, and collect, organize, and display relevant data to answer them	✳ Design investigations to address a question, and consider how data-collection methods affect the nature of the data set; ✳ Collect data using observations, surveys, and experiments; ✳ Represent data using tables and graphs, such as line plots, bar graphs, and line graphs; ✳ Recognize the differences in representing categorical and numerical data.
Select and use appropriate statistical methods to analyze data	✳ Describe the shape and important features of a set of data, and compare related data sets, with an emphasis on how the data is distributed; ✳ Use measures of center, focusing on the median, and understand what each does and does not indicate about the data set; ✳ Compare different representations of the same data and evaluate how well each representation shows important aspects of the data.
Develop and evaluate inferences and predictions that are based on data	✳ Propose and justify conclusions and predictions that are based on data, and design studies to further investigate the conclusions or predictions.
Understand and apply basic concepts of probability	✳ Describe events as likely or unlikely and discuss the degree of likelihood using such words as *certain, equally likely,* and *impossible;* ✳ Predict the probability of outcomes of simple experiments and test the predictions; ✳ Understand that the measure of the likelihood of an event can be represented by a number from 0 to 1.

NCTM Standards
Data Analysis and Probability
Grades 6–8

Standards	Expectations
Formulate questions that can be addressed with data, and collect, organize, and display relevant data to answer them	✳ Formulate questions, design studies, and collect data about a characteristic shared by two populations or different characteristics within one population; ✳ Select, create, and use appropriate graphical representations of data, including histograms, box plots, and scatterplots.
Select and use appropriate statistical methods to analyze data	✳ Find, use, and interpret measures of center and spread, including mean and interquartile range; ✳ Discuss and understand the correspondence between data sets and their graphical representations, especially histograms, stem-and-leaf plots, box plots, and scatterplots.
Develop and evaluate inferences and predictions that are based on data	✳ Use observations about differences between two or more samples to make conjectures about the populations from which the samples were taken; ✳ Make conjectures about possible relationships between two characteristics of a sample on the basis of scatterplots of the data and approximate lines of fit; ✳ Use conjectures to formulate new questions, and plan new studies to answer them.
Understand and apply basic concepts of probability	✳ Understand and use appropriate terminology to describe complementary and mutually exclusive events; ✳ Use proportionality and a basic understanding of probability to make and test conjectures about the results of experiments and simulations; ✳ Compute probabilities for simple compound events, using such methods as organized lists, tree diagrams, and area models.

1. Share a graph, chart, or table with students every day. Begin by interpreting the data and gradually turn that task over to your students.

2. Choose data collection, organization, and interpretation topics that will interest students. Create a desire to know!

3. Assign survey projects to involve students in data collection and subsequent representation of the data.

4. Engage students in group projects that give them choices of how to represent data. Then have them explain their decisions and work to others.

5. Encourage students to collect graphs, charts, and tables from magazines, newspapers, advertisements, etc.

6. Make the teaching of central tendency relevant by using mean, median, mode, and range as a part of each assessment debriefing. Students will learn what has relevance to them!

SUPER SUCCESS STRATEGIES

1. Be *aware* of all the data collecting, organizing, and interpreting that happens in our daily lives.

2. *Look closely* when you see graphs, charts, and tables. Try to figure out what they mean.

3. Before attempting to answer questions about a graph, chart, or table, *study what you are given* very closely. Read all the titles, captions, and labels. On graphs, make sure you understand what the horizontal and vertical axes represent.

4. *Look for keys* that show quantities. For instance, a symbol might represent 1000 items rather than one.

5. *Read questions very carefully* to understand what is being asked about the information given.

Data Analysis (4–5)

Test	pages 126–127										
	1	2	3	4	5	6	7	8	9	10	11
CAT	X					X	X				X
IOWA	X	X				X	X				X
MAT7						X		X	X	X	
SAT9	X					X	X	X		X	X
Terra	X					X	X				X
FCAT										X	
ESPA	X	X			X		X				X
ISAT			X	X						X	
LEAP						X					
MEAP						X					
NYS	X		X				X			X	X
PACT		X	X	X							
TAAS						X					

Data Analysis (6–8)

Test	pages 128–129												pages 130				
	1	2	3	4	5	6	7	8	9	10	11	12	1	2	3	4	5
CAT	X						X	X	X	X	X	X	X	X	X	X	X
IOWA	X	X					X	X	X	X	X	X	X	X	X	X	X
MAT7	X						X	X	X	X	X	X	X	X	X	X	X
SAT9							X	X	X	X	X	X	X	X	X	X	X
Terra						X	X	X	X	X	X	X	X	X	X	X	X
FCAT										X	X	X	X	X	X	X	X
GEPA						X	X	X	X	X	X	X	X	X	X	X	X
ISAT							X	X	X	X	X	X	X	X	X	X	X
LEAP							X	X	X	X	X	X	X	X	X	X	X
MCAS			X			X	X	X	X					X	X	X	X
MEAP							X	X	X	X	X	X	X	X	X	X	X
NYS														X	X	X	X
PACT			X														
TAAS			X	X	X					X	X	X	X	X	X	X	X

Grades 4–5

Data Analysis

To find the mean …

Choose the correct answer for each problem.

1. Dory took her test scores home. The scores were 81, 77, 91, 86, 95. Her mom asked her to find her test average. What was the mean average of her scores?
- Ⓐ 78
- Ⓑ 80
- Ⓒ 82
- Ⓓ 86

2. Which group of numbers has the greatest mean average?
- Ⓕ 5, 6, 7
- Ⓖ 3, 9, 8
- Ⓗ 2, 7, 4
- Ⓙ 2, 9, 8

3. Which is larger, the mode or the mean of the following numbers?

   8, 12, 14, 8, 8, 11, 15, 12
- Ⓐ mean
- Ⓑ mode
- Ⓒ There are 2 modes.
- Ⓓ They are the same.

4. What is the median of the following numbers?

   3, 9, 6, 4, 5, 12, 10, 9, 8
- Ⓕ 9
- Ⓖ 8
- Ⓗ 7 $\frac{1}{2}$
- Ⓙ 5

5. Here are the temperature readings taken by Mr. Hoffman's class every hour of the school day last Thursday. What is the mode of this data?

   53° 57° 59° 58° 53° 51° 50°
- Ⓐ 58°
- Ⓑ 59°
- Ⓒ 50°
- Ⓓ 53°

Use this bar graph to answer questions 6–8.

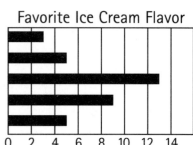

Favorite Ice Cream Flavor

vanilla
strawberry
chocolate
coffee
other

0 2 4 6 8 10 12 14

6. The students in the fifth grade after school program created this bar graph using their favorite ice cream flavors as the data. What is their favorite?
- Ⓕ strawberry
- Ⓖ chocolate
- Ⓗ coffee
- Ⓙ other

7. What is the mean of the different flavor choices voted on by the students?

(A) 5

(B) 6

(C) 7

(D) 8

8. What is the range of the data?

(F) 3 to 13 students

(G) 3 to 5 students

(H) 3 to 14 students

(J) 0 to 13 students

Use this pictoral graph to answer questions 9–11.

Number of Compact Discs Sold in 1 Year

Music World	⊙⊙⊙⊙⊙⊙⊙⊙
Aladin Music	⊙⊙⊙⊙⊙⊙
Sing Song	⊙⊙⊙⊙⊙
Larry's Rock	⊙⊙⊙⊙⊙⊙⊙⊙⊙

Each ⊙ = 1000 CD's

9. How many more CD's were sold by Music World than Sing Song?

(A) 30

(B) 300

(C) 3000

(D) 30,000

10. Which of the four music stores shown on the graph sold the most compact discs?

(F) Music World

(G) Aladdin Music

(H) Sing Song

(J) Larry's Rock

11. What was the mean number of CD's sold by the four music stores in one year?

(A) 4000

(B) 5000

(C) 7000

(D) 20,000

Grades 6–8

Data Analysis

To find the mean ...

Choose the correct answer for each problem.

1. Which graph shows temperature going up over time?

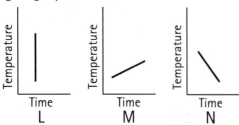

Ⓐ L
Ⓑ M
Ⓒ N
Ⓓ Both M and N

Mr. Lamb teaches 4 classes of geography. This bar graph shows the number of students in each class. Use the graph to answer questions 2–4.

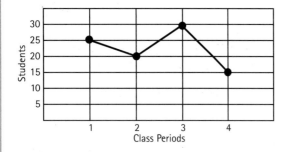

2. Lunch period is between third and fourth periods. How many students does Mr. Lamb teach before lunch?
Ⓕ 15
Ⓖ 30
Ⓗ 50
Ⓙ 75

3. How many students does Mr. Lamb teach altogether in the 4 geography classes?
Ⓐ 30
Ⓑ 60
Ⓒ 90
Ⓓ 120

4. In which two classes could Mr. Lamb have groups of three with no leftover students?
Ⓕ 1 and 2
Ⓖ 2 and 3
Ⓗ 1 and 4
Ⓙ 3 and 4

A local music store kept track of the 5 most frequently purchased types of CD's during April. The sales in all 5 categories totaled 240. Use the circle graph to answer questions 5-8.

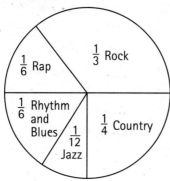

5. How many country CD's were purchased in April?
   Ⓐ 40   Ⓒ 80
   Ⓑ 60   Ⓓ 100

6. Which two music categories combined sold the same amount as Rock?
   Ⓕ Rap and Country
   Ⓖ Rap and Jazz
   Ⓗ Rap and R and B
   Ⓙ jazz and Country

7. How many Jazz and Rap CD's were sold in April?
   Ⓐ 40   Ⓒ 80
   Ⓑ 60   Ⓓ 100

8. How many more Rhythm and Blues CD's were sold than Jazz CD's?
   Ⓕ 20   Ⓗ 60
   Ⓖ 40   Ⓙ 80

Tim kept track of his quiz grades during the last grading period. Use the bar graph to answer questions 9-12.

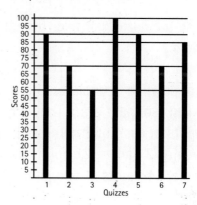

9. What is the range of Tim's scores?
   Ⓐ 55 – 85
   Ⓑ 55 – 100
   Ⓒ 70 – 90
   Ⓓ 0 – 100

10. What is the mean average of Tim's scores?
    Ⓕ 55   Ⓗ 80
    Ⓖ 70   Ⓙ 90

11. What is the median of Tim's scores?
    Ⓐ 55   Ⓒ 85
    Ⓑ 70   Ⓓ 90

12. If Tim's teacher decides to drop the lowest quiz grade, about how many points would Tim's mean average improve?
    Ⓕ 4
    Ⓖ 10
    Ⓗ 80
    Ⓙ 84

Grades 6–8

Data Analysis

To figure the range . . .

Choose the correct answer for each problem.

1. Wando High School had a terrific football season last year. They scored 27 points in each of 3 games, 32 points in each of 2 games, 21 points in one game, 14 points in one game, and 36 points in their last game. What is the mean average number of points they scored per game?
   Ⓐ 21 points
   Ⓑ 27 points
   Ⓒ 30 points
   Ⓓ 32 points

2. Choose the set of numbers that has the greatest range.
   Ⓕ 13, 17, 30
   Ⓖ 1, 6, 7
   Ⓗ 22, 28, 40
   Ⓙ 15, 21, 38

3. Kim's mom asked her to figure out her test average in social studies. Her test scores are 86, 79, 98, and 77. What is her mean average?
   Ⓐ 80
   Ⓑ 85
   Ⓒ 90
   Ⓓ 95

4. Joey kept track of how much he grew every 3 months for a year. From January through March, he grew $\frac{1}{2}$ inch, from April through June he grew $\frac{1}{4}$ inch, from July through September he grew $\frac{3}{4}$ inch, and from October through December he grew $1\frac{1}{8}$ inch. What was his average growth for a 3 month period during the year?
   Ⓕ $\frac{1}{4}$ inch
   Ⓖ $\frac{11}{32}$ inch
   Ⓗ $\frac{21}{32}$ inch
   Ⓙ $\frac{3}{4}$ inch

5. Anthony earned an average of $42 a week for two weeks. The second week he earned $46. How much did he earn the first week?
   Ⓐ $41
   Ⓑ $40
   Ⓒ $39
   Ⓓ $38

Probability and Combinations

*t*oo often probability is a topic that is left out of our elementary and middle school curriculum. It is typically at the end of textbooks or tacked on almost as an afterthought. This doesn't need to deter us from presenting it to our students! We can teach probability all year long and use everyday settings to make it come alive for kids. Because probability is simply the likelihood of events occurring, we can integrate probability into lessons on weather, asking students to listen to forecasts and talk about what the weather person means when she says there is a 20% chance of rain. Getting heads or tails on a penny toss, drawing a certain card from a deck, predicting what a spinner will land on in a favorite game—all are examples of probability. We should help students recognize independent and dependent choices throughout the school year. An actual probability unit isn't necessary to teach these basic concepts!

TEACHING TIPS

1. Approach probability and combinations from a "real world" standpoint. Use scenarios that have meaning for students. For instance, discuss the probability of outcomes of tossing dice in a Monopoly game.

2. Give students lots of hands-on practice. Have them flip coins, spin spinners, make random choices, etc., in pairs or groups. Encourage them to have fun with it!

3. Rather than just giving rules for determining combinations, have students manipulate concrete items to discover how to determine combinations. For instance, if the question involves creating outfits from 3 blouses and 2 skirts, have the actual items in the classroom to use as discovery tools.

4. Probability and combinations fit naturally throughout the math curriculum, due in part to how much they relate to practical situations. Don't wait until the end of the school year to approach the subject!

Probability and Combinations

1. *Dealing with probability and combinations is not a mystery!* Look for examples in class and find others on your own to help make sense of it all.

2. Read and imagine probability items carefully. *Picture in your mind* what the event looks like.

3. If you are given a spinner, examine how the circle is divided up. *Are all the pie shapes the same size?* If one is larger, chances are that the spinner will land on it more often, no matter how many times it is spun.

4. In *spinner items*, look carefully at how the pie shapes are labeled. For instance, is there more than one *A* or more than one *3*? This will change how you think about the chances of landing on a particular pie shape.

5. Remember that the chances of a *random event* happening depends on how many ways it could happen divided by the *total number* of possibilities. For example, the chances of choosing a red marble when blindfolded if there are four red marbles in a group of seven marbles would be four divided by seven, or $\frac{4}{7}$.

6. When dealing with *combinations*, multiply the number of basic things by the number of things they could be combined with. For instance, if you have 3 shirts that could be put with 4 pairs of shorts, multiple 3 times 4 to get 12 possible combinations.

7. *Watch for words* like *even* and *odd* and *multiples of 3* that might limit what you are looking for.

Probability and Combinations (4–5)

Test	pages 134–135											
	1	2	3	4	5	6	7	8	9	10	11	12
CAT				X	X							
IOWA						X						
MAT7	X	X	X									
SAT9		X				X	X	X	X			
Terra	X	X				X			X			
FCAT							X					
ESPA												X
ISAT									X		X	X
LEAP												
MCAS	X	X					X	X		X	X	
MEAP												
NYS				X		X	X	X	X			X
PACT												
TAAS	X	X				X					X	X

Probability and Combinations (6, 7, 8)

Test	pages 135–136												page 137						
	1	2	3	4	5	6	7	8	9	10	11	12	1	2	3	4	5	6	7
CAT							X	X			X								
IOWA									X										
MAT7								X			X								
SAT9																			
Terra																			X
FCAT								X			X		X		X	X			
GEPA			X		X						X			X					X
ISAT											X						X		
LEAP	X																	X	
MCAS		X			X					X				X					
MEAP	X																X	X	
NYS				X							X		X					X	X
PACT																			
TAAS					X	X				X			X						

Grades 4–5

Probability and Combinations

The spinner will probably land on . . .

Choose the correct answer for each problem.

1. Amy is showing her cousin a game she plays using a spinner. If she spins the arrow 7 times, which letter will it probably stop on most often?
   - Ⓐ E
   - Ⓑ F
   - Ⓒ G
   - Ⓓ H

2. If this spinner is spun 5 times, which letter will it probably point to the least number of times?
   - Ⓕ N
   - Ⓖ M
   - Ⓗ L
   - Ⓙ K

3. Jamal wrote each letter of the word *telephone* on a card and placed them face down on the table. If Garrett chooses a card, what is the probability that he will choose an *e*?
   - Ⓐ $\frac{1}{2}$
   - Ⓑ $\frac{1}{3}$
   - Ⓒ $\frac{1}{4}$
   - Ⓓ $\frac{1}{6}$

4. A number cube has six faces numbered 1–6. A roll that shows an even number on the face that is up allows the player to move. What is the probability on one roll that Shantelle will get to move?
   - Ⓕ $\frac{1}{2}$
   - Ⓖ $\frac{2}{6}$
   - Ⓗ $\frac{3}{6}$
   - Ⓙ $\frac{4}{6}$

5. A spinner game can be won by landing on a 2 or 3 on the game board. What are the chances of winning with one spin?
   - Ⓐ $\frac{2}{8}$
   - Ⓑ $\frac{3}{8}$
   - Ⓒ $\frac{4}{8}$
   - Ⓓ $\frac{6}{8}$

6. On which number is the spinner most likely to land?
   - Ⓕ 2
   - Ⓖ 3
   - Ⓗ 4
   - Ⓙ 5

7. Sophia has started a small business making jewelry with colored glass beads. She can make necklaces, bracelets, and earrings with either blue, red, green, or pink beads. How many different items in solid colors can she make?

Ⓐ 3
Ⓑ 6
Ⓒ 9
Ⓓ 12

8. Alexander is going on a trip. He plans to take 4 shirts, 2 pairs of jeans, and 3 pairs of shoes. How many outfits could he make?

Ⓕ 36
Ⓖ 24
Ⓗ 9
Ⓙ 4

9. What are the chances the spinner will land on a vowel?

Ⓐ $\frac{4}{8}$
Ⓑ $\frac{3}{8}$
Ⓒ $\frac{2}{8}$
Ⓓ $\frac{1}{8}$

10. A number cube has 6 faces, each with a number 1–6. If Annie tosses the cube 3 times and adds the 3 faces that appear, what is the highest total she could get?

Ⓕ 24
Ⓖ 21
Ⓗ 18
Ⓙ 15

11. Zander tossed a coin 4 times and it landed with heads, heads, tails and heads facing up. What is the probability that tails will be face up on the fifth toss?

Ⓐ one out of three
Ⓑ one out of two
Ⓒ two out of two
Ⓓ two out of three

12. Carmen's game of Chinese Checkers is missing some marbles. She only has 12 red, 10 green, 9 blue, 7 black and 5 white in her game bag. If she chooses one from the bag without looking, what is the probability she will choose a blue one?

Ⓕ $\frac{9}{9}$
Ⓖ $\frac{9}{43}$
Ⓗ $\frac{43}{9}$
Ⓙ $\frac{34}{43}$

Name _____

Grades 6–8

Probability and Combinations

The probability is . . .

Choose the correct answer for each problem.

1. If a coin is tossed 8 times and it comes up tails each time, what is the probability that the next time will be a head?

Ⓐ $\frac{1}{8}$ Ⓒ $\frac{3}{8}$
Ⓑ $\frac{1}{4}$ Ⓓ $\frac{1}{2}$

2. Marcus flips a penny, a dime, and a quarter at the same time. What is the probability that all 3 will land on heads?

Ⓕ $\frac{1}{2}$ Ⓗ $\frac{1}{8}$
Ⓖ $\frac{1}{3}$ Ⓙ $\frac{1}{9}$

3. If a coin is tossed 3 times, what is the probability that it will land on heads all 3 times?

Ⓐ $\frac{1}{2}$ Ⓒ $\frac{1}{8}$
Ⓑ $\frac{1}{3}$ Ⓓ $\frac{1}{9}$

4. If the numbers 1–8 are each written on 8 separate slips of paper, what is the probability that one slip drawn randomly will be 4 or less?

Ⓕ $\frac{1}{8}$ Ⓗ $\frac{4}{1}$
Ⓖ $\frac{1}{4}$ Ⓙ $\frac{1}{2}$

5. Each letter in the words *high school* is on a separate piece of paper. If one piece of paper is picked at random, what is the probability the letter on the paper will be an H?

Ⓐ $\frac{1}{10}$ Ⓒ $\frac{1}{3}$
Ⓑ $\frac{1}{5}$ Ⓓ $\frac{3}{10}$

6. Every Friday, Mr. Jennings draws a name from a box containing a slip of paper for each of the students in his fifth period class. The name drawn gets to choose the topic of class discussion. Last Friday, Jan's name was drawn and she chose the topic. Her name was put back in the box along with her 23 classmates. What is the probability Jan's name will be drawn again this Friday?

Ⓕ 1 in 23   Ⓗ 0 in 24
Ⓖ 1 in 24   Ⓙ 1 in 12

7. Two classes are working together on a probability experiment. Mr. Williams' class is made up of 14 boys and 16 girls. Mrs. Landry's class is made up of 10 boys and 15 girls. The students write their names on separate slips of paper. The teachers ask them to predict the probability of drawing a boy's name if the name is drawn from a box blindly. What is the probability?

Ⓐ $\frac{10}{25}$ Ⓒ $\frac{25}{30}$

Ⓑ $\frac{2}{11}$ Ⓓ $\frac{24}{55}$

8. Jesse's mom has an odd collection of silverware that has accumulated in the drawer in the kitchen. There are 16 spoons altogether with 3 that are sterling silver, 8 that have gold trim, and 5 that are stainless steel. If she reaches in without looking to get a spoon to stir the gravy, what is the probability that she will get a spoon with gold trim?

Ⓕ $\frac{1}{8}$ Ⓗ $\frac{1}{4}$

Ⓖ $\frac{3}{16}$ Ⓙ $\frac{1}{2}$

9. Seven friends shook hands with *each other* three times. How many times did one friend shake hands?

Ⓐ 3   Ⓒ 18

Ⓑ 7   Ⓓ 24

10. Alex is trying to understand the concepts of simple probability. Just reading about it is not enough. His teachers gave him a number cube with the six faces labeled 1–6. His teacher said that he should toss the cube 96 times and record the results on a chart. It is likely that the number cube will show 3 ____ times.

Ⓕ 3   Ⓗ 36

Ⓖ 16   Ⓙ 60

11. The Dolphins Team at Laing Middle School is concerned that their spring picnic at the park will be rained out Friday because the weather forecaster said there's a 25% probability that it will rain. What is the probability that it will not rain?

Ⓐ $\frac{1}{4}$ Ⓒ $\frac{3}{4}$

Ⓑ $\frac{1}{2}$ Ⓓ $\frac{4}{4}$

12. The six faces of a number cube are labeled with the numbers 1–6. What are the odds against rolling a 4?

Ⓕ $\frac{1}{4}$ Ⓗ $\frac{4}{6}$

Ⓖ $\frac{1}{6}$ Ⓙ $\frac{5}{6}$

Grades 6–8

Probability and Combinations

To find the number of possible combinations...

1. When the yearbook staff had to decide on the cover for the year, they could choose among 5 colors, 12 type designs, and 3 cover textures. From how many different combinations could they choose?
   - (A) 180
   - (B) 60
   - (C) 20
   - (D) 12

2. Sabrina bought 4 pairs of shorts and 7 shirts on her vacation. How many different outfits (combinations) could she make?
   - (F) 7
   - (G) 11
   - (H) 14
   - (J) 28

3. What are the odds that the spinner will land on an even number if it is spun once?
   - (A) 3 to 7
   - (B) 3 to 4
   - (C) 4 to 7
   - (D) 4 to 3

4. If a spinner is spun 200 times, using the rules of probability, about how many times would it land on 1?
   - (F) 25
   - (G) 50
   - (H) 100
   - (J) 200

5. If Alena spins the spinner 32 times, what is likely to happen?

   - (A) It will land on a vowel twice as often as a consonant.
   - (B) It will land on A twice as often as C.
   - (C) It will land on B as often as C.
   - (D) It will land on C twice as many times as B.

6. What is the probability that the spinner arrow will land on a multiple of 3?
   - (F) $\frac{4}{9}$
   - (H) $\frac{1}{2}$
   - (G) $\frac{1}{3}$
   - (J) $\frac{1}{9}$

7. If the spinner is spun twice, what is the probability it will land on 4 both times?
   - (A) $\frac{1}{2}$
   - (C) $\frac{1}{16}$
   - (B) $\frac{1}{4}$
   - (D) $\frac{1}{32}$

State Provided Tools

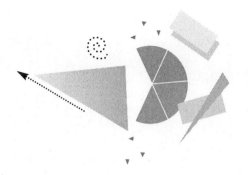

Many state standardized tests include math tools for students to use. These tools may be as simple as a list of formulas for finding areas of polygons or as elaborate as perforated protractors and rulers to be punched out and used during testing. Some states provide full pages of measurement equivalencies and formulas while others provide nothing. The nationally normed standardized tests rarely provide tools of any kind. Here are samples of what some states provide for students along with their tests.

Formula Chart

Perimeter	square rectangle	$P = 4s$ $P = 2(1 + w)$
Circumference	circle	$C = 2\pi r$
Area	square rectangle triangle trapezoid circle	$A = s^2$ $A = lw$ or $A = bh$ $A = bh/2$ $A = \frac{1}{2}(b^1 + b^2)h$ $A = 2\pi r^2$
Surface Area	cube cylinder (lateral)	$S = 6s^2$ $S = 2\pi rh$
Volume	rectangular prism cylinder cube	$V = lwh$ $V = \pi r^2h$ $V = s^3$
Pythagorean Theorem	right triangle	$a^2 + b^2 = c^2$

Measurement Conversions

	METRIC	CUSTOMARY
Length	1 kilometer = 1000 meters 1 meter = 100 centimeters 1 centimeter = 10 millimeters	1 mile = 1760 yards 1 mile = 5280 feet 1 yard = 3 feet 1 foot = 12 inches
Volume and Capacity	1 liter = 1000 milliliters	1 gallon = 4 quarts 1 gallon = 128 ounces 1 quart = 2 pints 1 pint = 2 cups 1 cup = 8 ounces
Weight	1 kilogram = 1000 grams 1 gram = 1000 milligrams	1 ton = 2000 pounds 1 pound = 16 ounces
Time		1 year = 12 months 1 year = 52 weeks 1 year = 365 days 1 week = 7 days 1 day = 24 hours 1 hour = 60 minutes 1 minute = 60 seconds

Answer Key

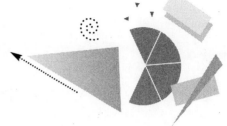

Chapter 1 Numbers and Operations
Place Value (4-5) p. 13
1. C
2. J
3. B
4. G
5. C
6. J
7. C
8. F
9. B

Place Value (6-8) p. 14
1. B
2. J
3. B
4. H
5. B
6. G
7. D
8. G
9. C

Comparing Whole Numbers, Fractions, and Decimals (4-5) p. 18
1. B
2. G
3. C
4. J
5. A
6. H
7. B
8. J
9. A
10. H
11. C
12. F
13. B
14. J
15. D
16. F
17. C
18. F

Comparing Whole Numbers, Fractions, and Decimals (4-5) p. 20
1. A
2. H
3. B
4. J
5. B
6. J

Comparing Whole Numbers, Fractions, and Decimals (6-8) p. 21
1. C
2. H
3. C
4. F
5. A
6. J
7. B
8. J
9. B
10. F
11. B
12. H
13. B
14. J
15. A
16. H

Computation with Whole Numbers, Fractions, and Decimals (4-5) p. 26
1. A
2. H
3. D
4. G
5. A
6. F
7. B
8. J
9. D
10. H
11. D
12. F
13. B
14. H

15. A
16. J
17. B
18. F
19. B
20. H
21. D
22. F
23. B

Computation with Whole Numbers, Fractions, and Decimals (6-8) p. 28
1. D
2. F
3. B
4. F
5. C
6. F
7. B
8. H
9. C
10. H
11. D
12. G
13. B
14. G
15. D
16. G
17. A
18. F
19. B
20. J
21. C
22. F
23. B

Problem Solving with Whole Numbers, Fractions, and Decimals (4-5) p. 33
1. C
2. G
3. A
4. H
5. B

6. H
7. C
8. H
9. B
10. J
11. C
12. G
13. D
14. F
15. B
16. J
17. C

Problem Solving with Whole Numbers, Fractions, and Decimals (6-8) p. 35
1. B
2. J
3. A
4. H
5. C
6. G
7. B
8. J
9. D
10. J
11. D
12. F
13. C

Computation and Problem Solving with Percent (6-8) p. 40
1. D
2. H
3. C
4. G
5. B
6. F
7. A
8. J
9. C
10. J
11. A
12. H
13. C
14. J
15. D
16. G
17. B
18. G

Computation and Problem Solving with Percent (6-8) p. 42
1. D
2. G
3. B
4. F

Ratio and Proportion (4-5) p. 45
1. B
2. F
3. B
4. H
5. C

Ratio and Proportion (6-8) p. 46
1. B
2. F
3. D
4. J
5. C
6. F
7. B
8. J
9. A
10. J
11. C
12. H
13. A
14. J
15. C

Expanded and Scientific Notation (6-8) p. 50
1. D
2. J
3. A
4. J
5. B
6. H
7. D
8. H

Multiples and Factors (4-5) p. 54
1. D
2. F
3. B
4. G
5. A
6. H
7. B
8. H
9. D
10. G
11. C
12. G
13. A
14. H
15. D

Multiples and Factors (6-8) p. 56
1. C
2. G
3. A
4. G

5. C
6. G
7. D
8. H
9. D
10. H
11. D
12. J
13. B
14. J
15. D

Estimation and Rounding (4-5) p. 61
1. C
2. H
3. A
4. G
5. D
6. F
7. D
8. H
9. B
10. G
11. D
12. G
13. A

Estimation and Rounding (6-8) p. 63
1. B
2. H
3. A
4. F
5. B
6. H
7. B
8. G
9. C
10. J
11. B
12. F
13. C
14. G
15. B
16. J

Order of Operations (6-8) p. 67
1. C
2. G
3. B
4. J
5. B

Integers (6-8) p. 70
1. A
2. G
3. C
4. H
5. A
6. J
7. A
8. G
9. C
10. G
11. C
12. G
13. C
14. F
15. B
16. H
17. A
18. F
19. B
20. H

Working with Variables (4-5) p. 78
1. C
2. G
3. D
4. G
5. C
6. G
7. C
8. H
9. C
10. J
11. B
12. G
13. D
14. G
15. A

Working with Variables (6-8) p. 80
1. C
2. G
3. A
4. G
5. C
6. H
7. C
8. J
9. B
10. G
11. B
12. H
13. D
14. J
15. D
16. J

17. C
18. H

Patterns (4-5) p. 84
1. B
2. H
3. B
4. J
5. C
6. F
7. D
8. H
9. B
10. F
11. D
12. G

Patterns (6-8) p. 86
1. B
2. G
3. D
4. J
5. B
6. G
7. C

Perimeter and Area (4-5) p. 93
1. C
2. J
3. C
4. G
5. D
6. H
7. A
8. F
9. C
10. H
11. B
12. G
13. C

Perimeter and Area (4-5) p. 95
1. F
2. B
3. H
4. B

Perimeter and Area (6-8) p. 96
1. D
2. F
3. D
4. H
5. A
6. J
7. D
8. H

9. B
10. J
11. D
12. H
13. D

Perimeter and Area (6-8) p. 98
1. J
2. A
3. G
4. A

Angles and Their Measurement (4-5) p. 100
1. C
2. G
3. C
4. H

Angles and Their Measurement (6-8) p. 101
1. A
2. J
3. C
4. J
5. A
6. G
7. C
8. G
9. A
10. G
11. A
12. H

Assorted Topics in Geometry (4-5) p. 105
1. C
2. J
3. A
4. J
5. C
6. J
7. B
8. F
9. D
10. H
11. B
12. J
13. B

Assorted Topics in Geometry (4-5)
p. 107
1. G
2. D
3. F
4. D
5. H
6. A

Assorted Topics in Geometry (6-8)
p. 108
1. D
2. J
3. D
4. G
5. D
6. J
7. B
8. G
9. C
10. J
11. A
12. J
13. D
14. F
15. D

Assorted Topics in Geometry (6-8)
p. 110
1. G
2. D
3. F
4. B
5. H
6. D
7. J
8. B
9. G
10. B
11. G
12. B

Measurement (4-5) p. 117
1. C
2. F
3. B
4. G
5. D
6. F
7. B
8. H
9. D
10. G
11. C
12. H
13. D
14. H

15. C
16. F
17. A

Measurement (6-8) p. 119
1. A
2. J
3. C
4. J
5. C
6. H
7. D
8. J
9. B
10. G
11. A
12. F
13. C
14. J
15. D
16. H

Data Analysis (4-5) p. 126
1. D
2. G
3. A
4. G
5. D
6. G
7. C
8. F
9. C
10. J
11. C

Data Analysis (6-8) p. 128
1. B
2. J
3. C
4. J
5. B
6. H
7. B
8. F
9. B
10. H
11. C
12. F

Data Analysis (6-8) p. 130
1. B
2. J
3. B
4. H
5. D

Probability and Combinations
(4-5) p. 134
1. D
2. F
3. B
4. F
5. A
6. F
7. D
8. G
9. A
10. H
11. B
12. G

Probability and Combinations
(6-8) p. 136
1. D
2. H
3. C
4. J
5. D
6. F
7. D
8. J
9. C
10. G
11. C
12. J

Probability and Combinations
(6-8) p. 138
1. A
2. J
3. A
4. H
5. D
6. G
7. C